TYING NYMPHS

ESSENTIAL FLIES AND TECHNIQUES FOR THE TOP PATTERNS

CHARLIE CRAVEN

Published by

Headwater Books
PO Box 202
Boiling Springs, PA 17007
www.headwaterbooks.com

Printed in United States of America

First edition
ISBN: 978-1-934753-35-4
eBook ISBN: 978-1-934753-36-1

Cover and interior design by Gavin Robinson

Library of Congress Control Number: 2015945216

10 9 8 7 6 5

DEDICATION

For Lisa . . . you're kind of a big deal.

CONTENTS

ACKNOWLEDGMENTS

Writing a third book was no easy task. Without endless help and understanding from my family, friends, and coworkers, this book would never have been written. It is with this in mind that I want to thank a few folks specifically.

A giant thank you to Ross Bartholomay, Dave Cook, and Jay Zimmerman. These are the guys I work and fish with every day, and who put up with me being cranky after late nights in front of the laptop, camera, and vise, and they endure my endless questions regarding clarity of direction and favorite patterns. They are always good for a laugh or a slap in the face when I need it.

Thanks also go to my dear friend Brandon Patterson, who is not only incredibly fun to fish with but has a unique insight into fly patterns and tying that I just can't replicate. Your friendship and help over the years has been priceless.

No thanks at all to my buddy Matt Prowse, who, while always great fun and good for a boat ride full of laughs, hates nymph fishing and really had nothing to offer more than levity. Thanks for nothin', pal.

Special thanks to Chris Sparks and the lovely and talented Erin Block for proofreading this manuscript, providing me with sanity checks and an honest set of eyes and ears. If there is anything left out of this book, it sure isn't their fault.

Thanks to Robert Younghanz and George Daniel for clarifying sticky wordings and details in their respective fields of entomology and Euro-nymphing. It's really nice to have such a great community of people to work with who share as freely as you two.

Thank you to my editor, publisher, and friend, Jay Nichols, who has turned out to be the most patient man on earth in waiting for this manuscript, always gentle with the criticism and so easy to work with. I can't thank you enough for the opportunities you've given, my friend. You're in a class all your own.

To all five of my kids—Charlie, Jackson, Julie, Sam, and Jonathan—for their understanding and patience when their dad was distracted from everyday life in pursuit of what has become this book. Every one of you make my life better in more ways than you'll ever know and I love you all dearly. You mean more to me than any fish ever could.

And finally, a gigantic thank you and a big wet kiss (which she will wipe off immediately) to my wonderful wife, Lisa. I never could have finished this project without your unending support, grace, and patience. Your overwhelming confidence in me and understanding of how my crazy brain works has allowed me free rein to dig into this project while knowing that you've always got my back. I love you. You're my everything.

INTRODUCTION

Let's get one thing straight right off the bat: I know this book looks a lot like a pattern guide. I get it. I can understand why you'd be under that impression, what with the long table of contents listing some of the best flies anyone could fish or tie. But this book is not about fly patterns. This book is about fly-tying techniques—cleverly disguised, I might add, as some of the best nymph patterns around. You see, I have always thought of all fly tying as merely a collection of techniques, and the more of them you learn and master, the better you'll be at it. So many folks get hung up on learning patterns and don't pay enough attention to the techniques that go into them. Mastery of a wide variety of techniques is far more useful than simply parroting a bunch of different patterns.

I have put this book together to feature a slew of great nymph patterns, but the criteria I used went far beyond any individual pattern's fish-catching ability. The truth may hurt a little, but let's face it: Fish aren't that smart. There's no end to the stuff they'll put in their mouths, and while we like to fatten our egos with phrases like "tough fish" and "educated trout," they're really just simple little pea-brained critters that often willingly eat the little bits of fur and fluff we've assembled. I know that hurt to read. It's okay. You'll be alright.

This book aims to teach technique rather than highlight specific patterns, though there are a whole lot of really great fish-catching nymph patterns in this book. Flies like the Barr Emerger and the Soft-Hackle have been around for a long time and are insanely popular. Others, such as Jay Zimmerman's fantastic Ditch Damsel, are a bit more modern in their design elements, illustrating that there are several ways to skin a cat.

Do me a favor and pay close attention as you work your way through this book. I have not intended this volume as a beginning fly-tying manual, as I have already written that book. My intent is to expand on basic techniques and further expound on design elements and specific material applications. I've tried to include flies that feature interesting, useful techniques, design elements worth considering, and lastly, fish-catching ability. This is not to say that a single one of these patterns is not a proven fish catcher; it's just that so often it's the archer, not the arrow. I've tried to present a reasonable cross section of patterns tied to imitate the most prolific underwater bugs, some of them large and some tiny, all with the idea of passing worthy techniques on through these patterns. There are lots of ways to do everything and knowing a few different avenues can often get you there quicker and with more style.

I've purposely only skimmed over the various angling techniques used to fish most of these patterns. While nymph fishing is without a doubt the most effective way to catch fish, trying to broaden this book into a how-to-fish manual would just be too much. If you're interested in a wider range of fishing techniques and a more detailed description of them, I highly suggest George Daniel's great book, *Dynamic Nymphing*. George did a fantastic job with it and really explains the details of conventional nymphing, dry-and-dropper rigs, and the various aspects of European-style nymphing. Frankly, I think all anglers should read his book. It contains everything you'd ever want to know about nymph fishing and is full of great insights.

When it comes right down to it, we all have our own style of fishing and tying; to that end, what I present here is a pretty broad overview of what's out there, but it is in no way complete. The pattern selection was entirely up to me, and was based on the above criteria. I don't mean this to be a compendium of every possible technique or pattern, as I honestly believe that books like that become overwhelming. It'd be like making a cookbook with nothing but a description of every spice known to man and just leaving the reader to figure out when and how to use them. In being a bit more specific than that, this book will act as a guide to both the tying and fishing of a variety of great nymph patterns—and hey, learning a bunch of new techniques along the way makes it more fun for everyone. As always, the devil is in the details, so read through, pick a few patterns, and get started. Before long you'll not only have a pretty good handle on a wide range of techniques, you'll most likely end up with a few boxes full of flies.

1

BARR EMERGER

The Barr Emerger is not only a time-tested and proven pattern, tying it helps sharpen your skills on making smoothly tapered bodies, placement of materials, proportions, and overall shaping of the fly. The devil is in the details.

John Barr is, without a doubt, one of the most creative and innovative fly tiers in the world. With a long list of what are now "standard" patterns such as the Copper John, Slump Buster, and Vis-A-Dun to his credit, nearly everyone has some of John's influence in their fly box these days. John's Barr Emerger was one of his first commercial patterns; I believe this fly is nearly as old as I am. Developed on a Montana spring creek to match the half-hatched Pale Morning Duns (PMDs) that John found in the throat of a trout, this simple fly has taken on a few different iterations in recent years. These variations include a bead head version and a flashback version that can be tied to match both PMDs and Blue-Winged Olives (BWOs); it can be tied in both wet (tied on a TMC 2487) and dry (tied on a TMC 101) versions. The BWO version has become nothing short of a fly box staple over the years, and with good reason—it has never stopped working. A simple combination of basic materials tied to match the slim profile of a small mayfly nymph, the basic Barr Emerger lacks flash or sparkle or any of the other "add-ons" that are now so common. I believe it is this plainness that has produced the fly's successful

One of the keys to the Barr Emerger's effectiveness is its no-frills design. It is so simple, so plain, that fish don't get used to it, and it continues to work on pressured waters for sophisticated fish year in and year out.

track record. There's nothing out of line, nothing that can be considered too much—just drab colors, a slim, accurate profile, and a well-thought-out design that make this fly one that fish never seem to get wise to. I've often said JB is a fly-designing savant, and the Barr Emerger proves that over and over again.

Aside from being an incredible fish catcher, the Barr Emerger employs several tying techniques that can cross over and apply to other patterns as well. Tying and placing a sparse tail on a curved shank hook, building a smoothly tapered and proportioned abdomen, working with hackle fibers to form a wingcase and legs, and overlapping the wingcase and thorax onto the abdomen to provide a smooth overall shape are all highlights of the specific techniques used in this fly.

I have a few opinions when it comes to tying the Barr Emerger. It's been one of my favorite patterns for many years and it spent a lot of time tied to both my own and my clients' tippets back in the day. Because of that, I have tied more than my fair share of this pattern. When a pattern is working and you develop confidence in it, you also develop a few little tricks to tie them consistently.

I like to use brown spade hackle feather fibers for this fly's tails. Spade hackles are the odd-shaped feathers found on the outside edges of a dry-fly cape. Their fibers are stiff and they make excellent tails on dry flies as well. The feathers are slender and durable and match up well to the sparse tail of the natural. John clips these fibers to length—a step that, as a Type A kinda guy, has always rubbed me the wrong way. I've always figured you should just tie them the correct length to begin with, but after years of tying these to spec, I am finally not only comfortable with the square-cut tail, but have even grown to like it.

Spade hackles are found on all necks and are readily available. If you own a dry-fly neck, you own suitable spade hackles. Spades are found along the outside edge at the widest part of the neck and have a sort of funky shape. They used to be "spade" shaped, but as modern breeding techniques have produced feathers that are longer and skinnier, spades have become elongated as well. Essentially what we want are fibers that are long and stiff. You can absolutely use the fibers from a tailing pack, strung neck hackle, or even from a saddle, provided the fibers themselves are relatively stiff and long enough to work with.

I have had the good fortune to have known John Barr for many years now, and the even greater honor of tying and photographing all of his fly patterns for his groundbreaking 2006 book *Barr Flies.* As part of my assignment for this book, I tied each and every one of John's patterns to his specifications and, in some cases, with his own secret stash of custom materials. The custom dubbing mix John prefers for the Barr Emerger abdomen is not commercially available and is, frankly, a bit coarse for my liking on a small fly like this. I have found that olive-brown Superfine dubbing matches the original color quite well and is readily available at nearly any good fly shop. I use Adams gray Superfine for the thorax on the BWO version and pale yellow Superfine for the thorax on the PMDs. Feel free to change this up to better match the insects in your area if need be, but I have found that these two colors work wonderfully in my fishing.

I also prefer spade hackle for the wing case, for a couple of reasons. Spade feathers have long fibers that make tying them in, folding them over, and then folding them back for the legs a much easier proposition than it would be with shorter hackle fibers, plus they are stiff, hard, and durable. As a final tip for tying the Barr Emerger, particularly the BWO version, I'll offer that you really should get a spool of iron gray 8/0 Uni-Thread, as used by John himself. When you first look at this color thread, it appears almost black, but the combination of this dark gray thread with the dubbing in the abdomen and the thorax produces a fishy shade, something I have come to really appreciate.

While I have many opinions about why this fly does work and how it should be tied, I often remind myself of a little lesson I've learned over the years: "You don't know everything." John's fly works today, it worked yesterday, it worked thirty years ago, and it will still be catching fish thirty years from now. I have my opinions, but I'm not changing the fly.

FLASHBACK BARR EMERGER (PMD)

Hook: #16-22 TMC 2487
Thread: Light cahill 8/0 Uni
Tail: Brown spade hackle fibers
Abdomen: Olive brown Superfine
Flashback: Medium Mirage Tinsel
Wing case and Legs: Cream-colored spade hackle fibers
Thorax: Pale yellow Superfine or beaver fur

BARR EMERGER (BWO)

Hook: #16-22 TMC 2487
Thread: Iron gray 8/0 UNI
Tail: Brown spade hackle fibers
Abdomen: Olive-brown Superfine
Wing case and Legs: Dark dun spade hackle fibers
Thorax: Adams gray Superfine

1. Place the hook in the vise at a bit of a tilt with the eye down, leaving the hook bend exposed. Start the thread two eye lengths back from the hook eye and wrap a smooth thread base back to a point on the bend that is in line with the hook eye.

2. Peel the fluff and softer fibers off the base of a brown spade hackle feather and preen the remaining fibers so they stand out from the stem. Peel off about a dozen fibers, taking care to keep the tips relatively even.

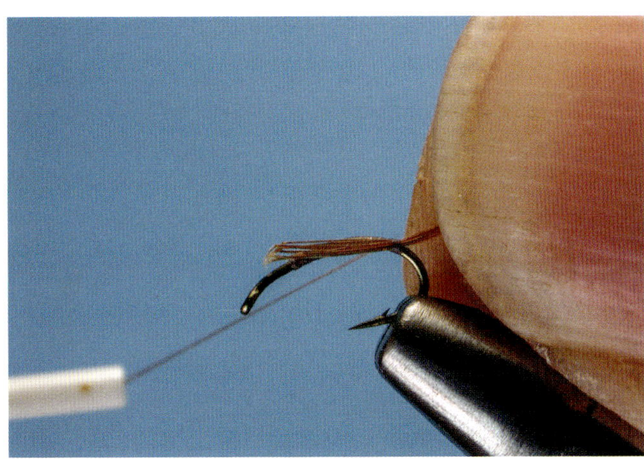

3. Bundle the spade hackle fibers up into a tidy bunch in your fingertips. Lay the butt ends of the spade fibers against the top of the shank at the bend and make a turn or two of thread over them. Make sure the fibers are anchored on the top of the hook. The tail length at this point is not important. Ultimately we will trim it to a length of about a half shank, so make sure it's at least a touch longer than that.

4. Wrap forward over the butt ends of the tails, leaving the tips of the fibers extending off the bend of the hook.

5. Continue wrapping forward over the butt ends of the tails. Because these butt ends did not extend past the hook eye, I was able to simply wrap over them and bury the ends under a smooth layer of thread; if they had been longer I would have needed to trim them short of the hook eye. Remount the hook in the vise as shown.

6. Dub a thin strand of olive-brown Superfine onto the thread. Use the bare thread between the dubbing and the hook to work smoothly back to the base of the tail (don't pile up a bunch of thread wraps at the bend waiting for the dubbing to come into play, as that will create a big, unsightly lump at the base of the tail) and make the first turn of dubbing come around the hook right at that point. The end of the dubbing is as thin as it's going to get, so we want that to be the start of the body taper.

7. Wrap the dubbing forward, building a smooth taper as you go. Bring the abdomen up to about two eye lengths back from the hook eye. Overlap the tying thread onto the front edge of the abdomen back to the 60/40 (abdomen/thorax) point on the shank.

8. Prep a dark dun spade hackle feather as you did with the brown for the tail. Peel twelve to eighteen fibers off the stem, taking pains to keep them even. Smaller flies won't need as many fibers as a larger fly. I am tying a size 16 here, so I have used eighteen fibers, but you'd be wise to scale that number down on smaller patterns to keep them properly proportioned.

9. Bundle the spade hackle fibers and lay them on the top of the hook where the thread is hanging. I try to tie these in relatively close to their butt ends so I have the maximum amount of working length left over for the wing case and legs. It doesn't really take a whole lot, but extra length makes the job easier. Capture the spade fibers with a few tight turns of thread at the 60/40 point on top of the front of the abdomen.

10. Wrap forward over the butt ends of the spade fibers to about an eye length back from the hook eye. Clip the excess butt ends flush and make a turn or two to bury them.

11. Dub a painfully thin strand of gray Superfine onto the thread. Most of the bulk needed for the thorax has already been created by the front end of the abdomen and the wing case tie-in, so think of this thin strand of dubbing as a layer of paint rather than filler. We just need to cover the area and add a bit of final shaping. Make the first turn of dubbing at the back of the index point and the next right behind it to work up the taper to the base of the wing case.

12. Starting at the index point and working up the tapered base will allow each turn of dubbing to hold the next in place and keep them from falling forward toward the hook eye, which is what happens if you try to dub down this taper from back to front. Work the dubbing smoothly back all the way to the wing case. This first layer will pretty much mirror the shape of the taper underneath it. We'll round it out a bit here in the next step.

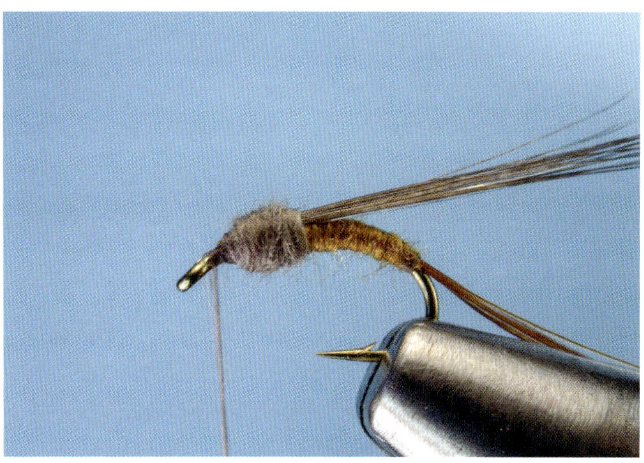

13. Work the dubbing forward from the base of the wing case to the back of the index point, squaring off the front end a bit and forming more of a ball shape. End with bare thread in that half an eye length behind the hook eye.

14. Grasp the wing case fibers and pull them forward over the top of the thorax. Try to keep them spread out a bit in your fingertips so they encompass the top of the fly and form a wide wing case.

15. While holding the tip ends of the wing case in your thread hand, reach over and take two wraps of thread using your material hand to anchor the wing case fibers down behind the hook eye. You can tug on the tips a bit more just to make sure you get the slack out. Once the wing case fibers are anchored down, take two more turns of thread over them, leaving the thread hanging at the back of the hook eye.

16. Press your thumbnail up against the base of the tips of the wing case right behind the hook eye hard enough to splay them.

17. Do your best to grab exactly half the fibers on the far side and pull them back along the near side of the shank, but rather than directly in line with the hook shank, hold them just slightly up.

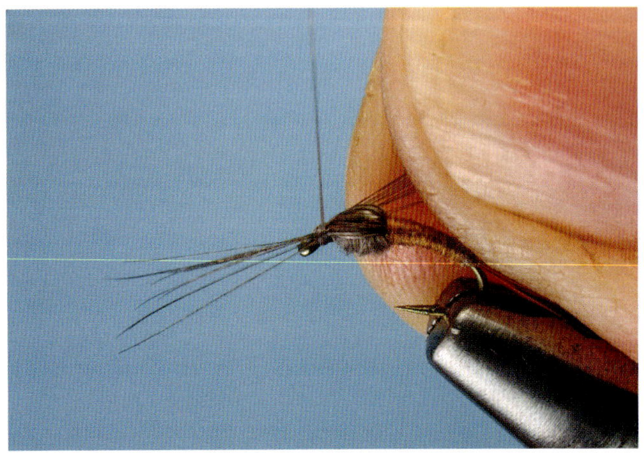

18. Capture the folded fibers under two or three tight wraps of thread that travel toward the rear of the head. This locks the legs back along the side of the fly. Thread torque should pull these fibers down slightly and center them along the far side of the hook shank. Don't make any more turns than necessary here to prevent a bulky head area.

19. Sweep the other half of the fibers back along the near side, but hold these ever so slightly low to allow the turn of thread to pull them up as you wrap over them. Again, make just a few turns to lock the near-side legs in place to manage bulk.

20. Once the legs are locked in place, do not make any more thread wraps. The thread head will be formed mostly by the existing bulk and the whip-finish. Reposition the hook to make the front end of the hook more level. This helps prevent the thread from falling off the downward sloping eye. It only has to happen to you 812 times before you realize you can do this. I'll save you the trouble.

21. Whip-finish, forming the final layer of thread on the head, and clip the thread.

22. Push the legs back along the fly and trim them about a scissor blade's width longer than the wing case. If you butt your scissor blades up to the wing case and make the cut straight across, you'll be perfect.

23. Tilt the hook in the vise, or remove it and just hold it in your fingers, to trim the tail square across and about a half shank length long.

2

BIOT EMERGER

The Biot Emerger will hone your skills in working with both biots and soft hen hackles. It is a versatile pattern to imitate mayfly and midge emergers year-round.

The Biot Emerger, from Colorado's Frying Pan River, was originally intended as a midge emerger pattern—a slim, handsomely segmented turkey biot body with a few dangling filaments of soft hackle at the front to imitate the midge's legs and sprouting wings. However, it also excels as an imitation for *Baetis* and other smallish mayflies, and I've even tied them up to a size 16 in yellow tones to imitate Pale Morning Duns. Because of this versatility, tying this pattern provides a quick, easy way to fill a couple of fly box needs, while at the same time getting more familiar with working with biots.

Biots come from the leading edge of a goose or turkey primary flight feather and are unlike most all other feathers. These short, hard fibers create lift to help these birds to fly and seeing a biot for the first time, you'd be hard pressed to even distinguish it as a feather. Their stiffness and tapered shape, however, lend them well to a variety of fly tying uses, from tails on Prince Nymphs and Copper Johns to bodies on flies like the Biot Emerger and even dry flies.

Turkey biots are my preferred material for flies like this, tied with the

While intended for use as a sunken nymph pattern, the Biot Emerger's soft-hackle collar and ribbed body create enough surface area to provide adequate flotation on flat water. Fish can take up feeding lies in some amazingly shallow water during a midge emergence.

ribbed edge standing up to create a three-dimensional segmentation. Turkey biots have a slightly longer standup edge, and this length makes the ribbing more prominent on the fly. This allows it to better imitate the gills found along the sides of the abdomen on a real mayfly nymph. It's easier to achieve the ribbed-abdomen look of this fly with the longer and easier-to-use turkey biots than it is with shorter goose biots, but goose will also work, particularly in the small sizes this fly is usually tied in. I find turkey biots to be slightly more pliable than goose biots, allowing easier overlap of their turns to help create a tapered body. Of course, you can certainly tie this fly with a smooth sided body by turning the biot over. Tying the biot in by the tip with the stand-up edge leading rather than following will create overlap to form a smooth ribbed body rather than the fuzzy, dimensional edge we'll get with the stand up edge leading. In this case, I would select goose biots as they have more prominent color contrast along their edges to create a more distinct ribbing.

Given the somewhat delicate nature of biot bodies in general, it's not a bad idea to wrap them over a thin layer of Zap-A-Gap to help toughen them up a bit. This additional step ensures biots can be used in creating tough, beautiful, and effective representations of the abdomens of both mayflies and midges. Once you get the hang of this technique it's easy to extrapolate it into other patterns like Biot Chironomids and even PoxyBack Stones.

There is no arguing with the look of a biot body, and with a few tricks the technique is simple to master. First, rather than trying to wrap the biots with my fingers, I use fine-tipped hackle tweezers made by Colorado's Robert Jorgensen. This tool allows me to place the wraps precisely and gives me a little extra length to work with in my fingers, and the tweezers hold on to fine feathers better than anything I've ever used. I find them priceless in this application and highly recommend them. I use these same tweezers to wrap the folded soft-hackle collar at the front of the fly too, and for the same reasons.

I have fished this pattern paired with various other nymphs on a conventional nymph rig with split shot and an indicator many times, but I find it even more effective as an upper water column emerger. To fish this fly shallower, I often fish it under a dry (such as a Parachute Adams) with no additional weight attached, and just let it find its way to the upper portion of the water column during a midge emergence. I have even greased the Biot Midge with floatant and fished it by itself when fish are taking midges off the surface.

Perhaps my favorite method of fishing the Biot Midge Emerger is under a small foam indicator with just a tiny bit of shot in shallow riffles. Fishing like this is as close as nymphing gets to dry-fly fishing, as you can often see the fish turn to take your fly. I rig the Emerger on the end of a 5X or 6X tippet with a small split shot (usually a number 8 or even a 9) about a foot above it. About three feet up from the weight, I place a foam Palsa indicator (or two)—more to act as a line marker than an actual strike indicator, but helpful in that area nonetheless. I'll fan-cast this rig throughout any available shallow riffles, covering the water as completely as possible and leaving nothing untouched.. The best features of this rig are that it casts so easily and is actually pretty stealthy. The small white foam indicator doesn't seem to raise any alarms, particularly in more broken riffled water, and I can often see the fish turning and flashing on the take, even if I'm not actually targeting sighted fish.

BIOT EMERGER (DUN)

Hook: #16-22 TMC 101
Thread: Black 8/0 Uni
Abdomen: Black turkey biot
Thorax: Black Superfine
Hackle: Medium dun hen neck hackle

BIOT EMERGER (BLACK)

Hook: #16-22 TMC 101
Thread: Black 8/0 Uni
Abdomen: Black turkey biot
Thorax: Black Superfine
Hackle: Black hen neck hackle

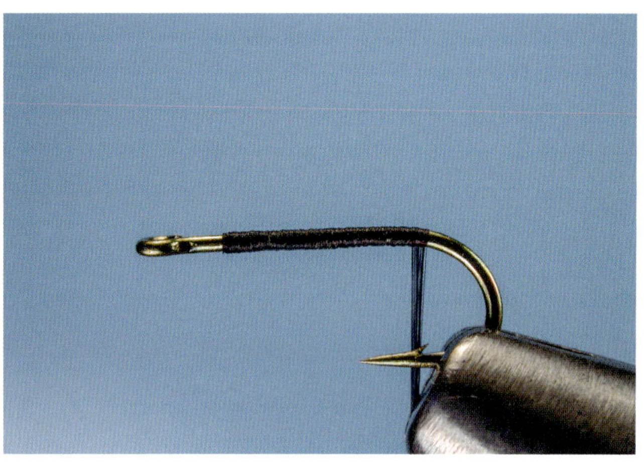

1. Start the thread about an eye length back from the eye and make a smooth thread base back to the bend.

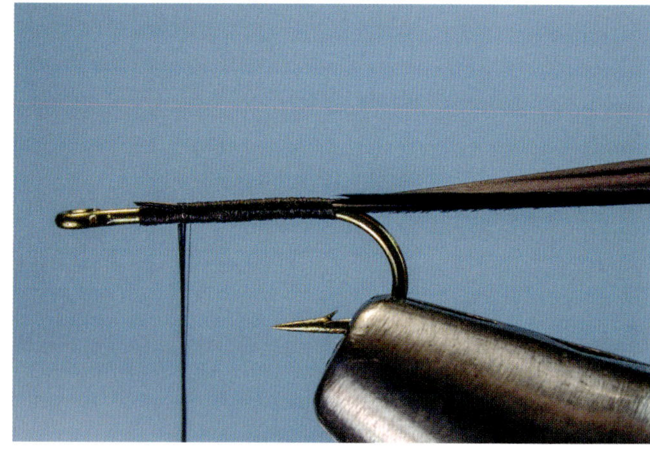

2. Tie in a black turkey biot by its tip with the raised edge facing down so that it will be the *following* edge on each wrap. In this case it doesn't make a huge difference if the biot comes from a right or left wing feather, as we will be wrapping it to form a stand-up rib and either way will work for this effect.

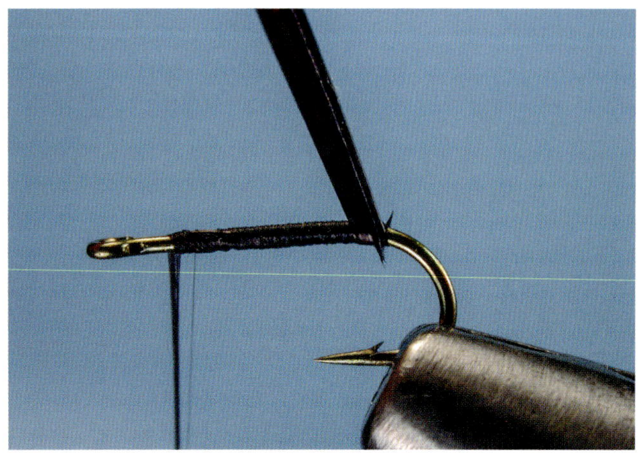

3. Grab the end of the biot in your hackle pliers and make the first turn around the bend of the hook. Look closely at this first turn. The stand-up edge of the feather should be on the back edge toward the bend, following the wrap rather than leading it. If yours isn't, untie it and turn it over.

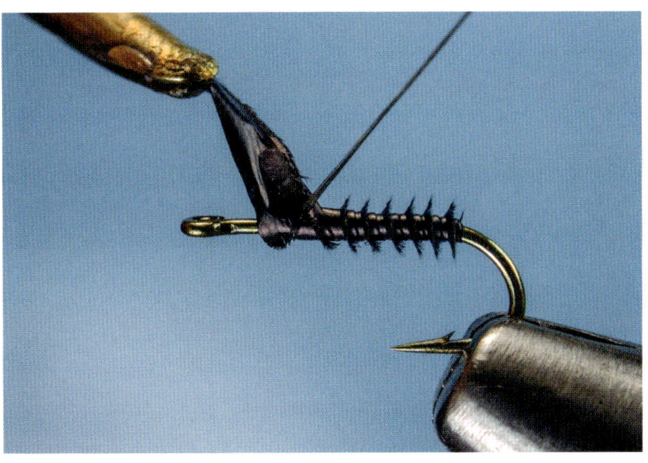

4. Continue spiraling the biot forward, overlapping the wraps slightly to create the ribbed body. Pull slightly forward on the biot and bring the thread at a sharp angle back over it. The base of the biot here at the front is fairly wide, so this long wrap will work much more cleanly to capture the end.

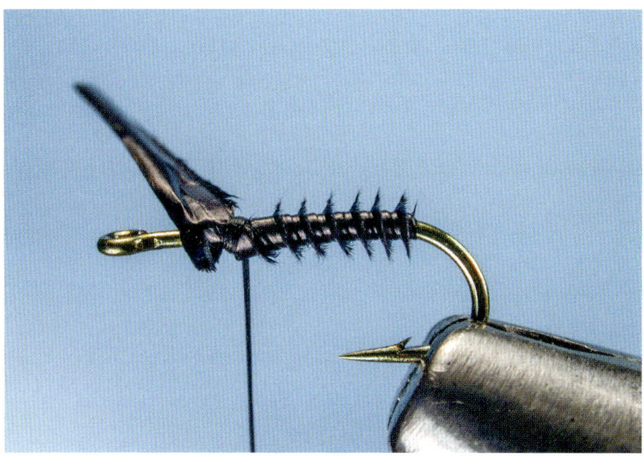

5. Cinch the wrap down and follow it up with a couple more to lock the front of the body down.

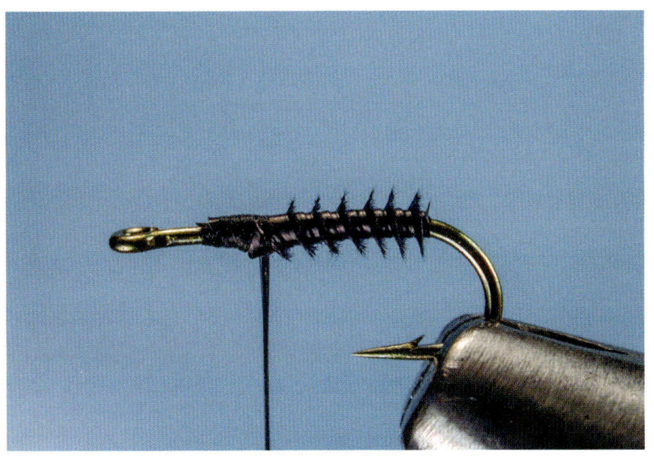

6. Trim the excess biot flush and make a few turns over the stub. Be sure you have a clean index point left at the front of the hook so you are not crowded later.

7. Build a small ball of black dubbing over the spot where you tied off the biot. Make sure you have an eye length worth of bare hook in front of the dubbing.

8. Now you can make a thread base from the front of the dubbing up to the hook eye and back again as a base for our hackle tie-in.

9. Select a hen neck feather that has barbs equal to about one and a half to two hook gaps. Clip the fluff from the bottom of the feather and prep the base by trimming the barbs short on either side. These little "teeth" will help hold the feather more securely while we fold and wrap it. You can just strip the stem and tie it in that way, but it will pull out most of the time and you'll need a bad-word thesaurus to get you through the rest of the day. Go ahead and trim them now.

10. Tie the hackle feather in by its butt at the back edge of the hook eye and wrap back over it to the base of the thorax. Make sure the inside (concave) side of the feather is facing the hook shank. This particular feather is trapped on the top of the hook shank, but it could just as easily be on the near, or even far side, of the hook. The main point here is that the inside of the feather's curve should face toward the hook shank.

11. Fold the hackle fibers back to one side. You only need about two turns of hackle here so don't feel like you need to do the whole feather unless it's for practice.

12. Make two turns of hackle, one in front of the other, up to the hook eye and tie the feather off with a couple turns of thread.

13. Clip the tip of the feather off flush.

14. With the thumb and forefinger of your thread hand, squeeze the hackle fibers down around the hook shank. While holding them in place, grab the tips with your free hand, taking care to keep them evenly distributed around the hook shank. Hold them down flat along the fly.

15. Make a few turns of thread over the front edge of the wrapped hackle to further slope it back and hold it in place. Make these wraps smooth and slightly tapered as this is also the thread head. These wraps should hold the hackle fibers back at a gentle slope a shown here. Whip-finish and clip the thread.

16. The finished fly should be slim and sparse. The colors can be varied to your heart's content, but I have found both the black version (shown here) and an all-gray version to be particularly effective. You can easily add some sparkle to this pattern by ribbing through the biot spacing with a single strand of pearl Krystal Flash, and a small glass or metal bead can be added as well.

3

CDC GOLDEN STONE

The CDC Stone is an unusual combination of materials that create a flowing profile. This pattern uses buoyant CDC in a weighted nymph pattern to create lifelike underwater movement and is a great primer for working with CDC on subsurface patterns.

Cul de canard, or CDC, is the term used for the small, soft feathers found around the preen gland of most waterfowl. These unusual feathers are widely used in dry-fly and emerger patterns because the helical nature of the fibers' radiating barbs and flues creates an enormous amount of surface area in a small space (their flotation has little to do with the preen oil itself). This keeps a fly floating low and well without adding excessive bulk.

The notion of using a buoyant feather like CDC on nymph patterns has really just started to catch on here in the United States, and I admit it struck me as an odd choice in the beginning. While most soft feathers lose their shape and mat together when wetted, CDC fibers have the unique ability to remain separated and trap air. This attribute makes it a great material for subsurface patterns as well as dry flies. Wetted CDC is lively and fluid in the

Adding a CDC collar to any nymph can give the fly a whole new look and often a slight fish-catching edge. The CDC Golden Stone is an excellent pattern across the United States.

water and creates movement and life unlike any other material I know of.

My first exposure to using CDC on nymph patterns came on a saltwater fishing trip several years back. One of the other guys on the trip happened to work at the old Kaufmann's Streamborn fly shop in Tigard, Oregon. While we were chatting and drinking after a day of fishing, we reverted to shop talk and trout fly patterns. He mentioned that one of the store's best-selling patterns was a bead head CDC Prince Nymph; I distinctly recall thinking to myself, "Well, that makes no sense." The notion of using CDC on a nymph pattern was completely odd and unheard of to me at that time, and I simply wrote it off as another one of those weird fly ideas I seem to be a magnet for.

It was many years later that I finally tied up a few CDC nymph patterns, namely a tungsten-beaded CDC Pheasant Tail, and stashed them away in my box. Their CDC collars were indeed pretty, and the basic Pheasant Tail chassis certainly had proven itself over the years, so I resolved to actually put them on my tippet that year and see just what they could do. Their maiden voyage into the drink was on Colorado's Arkansas River—and that trip made a believer out of me. Tied in sizes 10 and 12, my freshly tied CDC Pheasant Tails dredged fish after fish from deep runs, shallow riffles, and everything in between. The CDC collar swept back over the abdomen and thorax of the fly and created a lively halo of appendages that breathed and flowed in the currents, attracting fish far more effectively than the more plainly tied original.

Of course, having success with a new pattern immediately makes you start thinking about adaptations of the key features, and I started trying CDC on more and more nymph patterns. Bead Head Prince Nymphs, Soft Hackles, Pheasant Tails, and even Copper Johns can be spiced up with a CDC collar, lending themselves to even more applications. In the case of larger-profile mayfly nymphs, the addition of a CDC collar can replicate the emerging wings and dangling legs of the insect as it begins to hatch, or one that has become crippled and washed under the surface in the process. On flies like the Prince Nymph, the caddis emerger aspect is further highlighted with a ragged application of CDC in place of the traditional soft hen hackle collar. I encourage you to keep this simple variation in mind as you tie some of your favorite traditional patterns, and look for other places where it might be incorporated more effectively.

On smaller flies, the CDC fibers may be a bit too long and will need to be shortened. Do not trim them with your scissors into a square brush; instead, tear them off randomly to length with your thumbnail. We don't want a square-cut end on the CDC collar—we want random long and short fibers that will breathe and move nicely.

This CDC Golden Stone was one of the first original patterns I came up with using CDC on a subsurface bug. A couple simple turns at the front of an otherwise mundane Golden Stone Nymph pattern created life and movement without much work. The only downside to a CDC collar is that the feathers are generally pretty uniform in color when both natural and dyed, and have little to no variegation. I decided to face the CDC collar with a turn or two of dyed grizzly hen saddle to break up the collar pattern a bit, while maintaining the flowing look of the CDC. I have generally tied this pattern with a nice golden-colored synthetic dubbing from Trout Hunter, but realistically, it can be tied with nearly any of the coarser dubbings you might have, from synthetics to blends and even plain old dyed gold hare's mask dubbing. I do like to tie them heavily weighted and always with a tungsten bead, as I usually use them in a hopper/copper/dropper rig and the additional weight helps keep the whole rig down where it's supposed to be.

This fly also features a shellback of flash with a rib that creates a nicely segmented and attractive body that can be hijacked onto other patterns as well. Use your imagination and start recognizing the pieces as simply that—pieces and techniques that can be added into other flies to add to their design elements. As I've mentioned, the important part here is not the pattern, but rather the design aspect of using a material in a nontraditional application. The method of application is simple enough—nothing more than wrapping the feather like a conventional hen hackle feather, really—but the material itself being used in a new way is where great things come from. Try it.

This Williams Fork brown ate a Pheasant Tail with a CDC collar. Trim the CDC on smaller flies with your fingers, not scissors, for a more natural look.

CDC GOLDEN STONE

Hook: #8-14 TMC 5262
Thread: Yellow 6/0 Danville
Bead: Gold tungsten, sized to hook
Weight: Lead wire
Tail: Dyed yellow ring-necked pheasant tail fibers
Shellback: Opal Mirage Tinsel (large)
Rib: 3X tippet
Abdomen: Harrop Trout Hunter yellowish-tan Nymph/ Emerger dubbing
Thorax: Same as abdomen
Collar: Natural tan CDC and grizzly dyed gold hen saddle
Neck: Same as abdomen

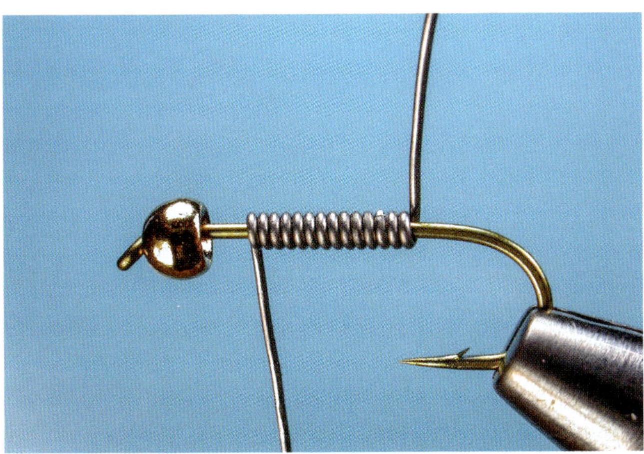

1. Place the bead on the hook and slide it up to the eye. Make a dozen or so turns of lead wire around the center of the shank and break off the stub ends.

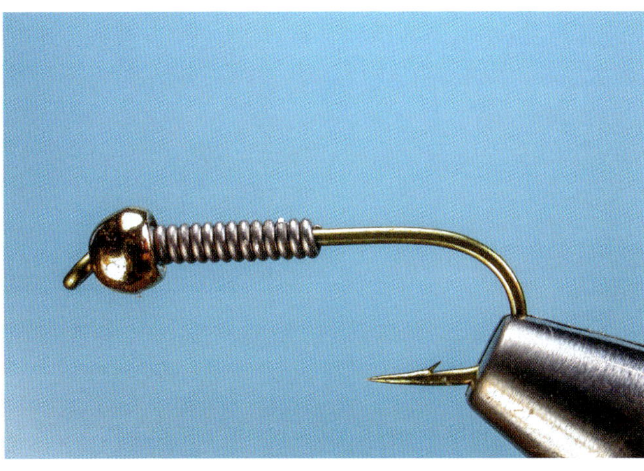

2. Press the lead wraps up into the recess in the back of the bead to hold it in place and center it on the hook.

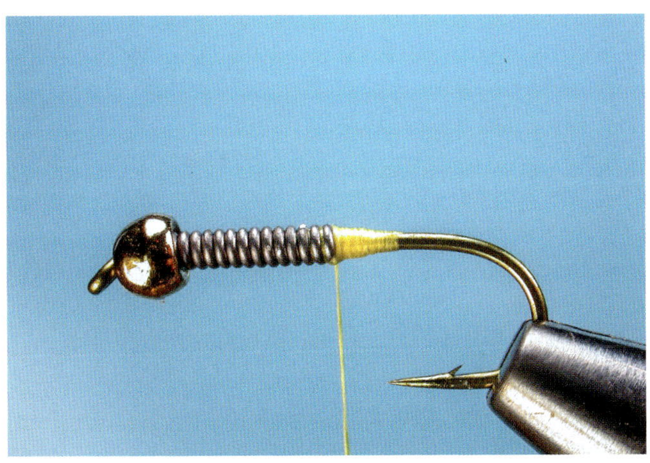

3. Start the thread at the back of the lead wraps and build a small thread dam from the bare shank up to the diameter of the lead. Try to make this transition as smooth as possible.

4. Continue wrapping the thread forward over the lead all the way up to the bead and then back again to the bend of the hook. Make another trip up and down the shank to anchor everything and form a smooth taper.

5. Preen about ten or twelve pheasant tail fibers out from the stem so that their tips become even. Peel these fibers from the stem and measure them to about a half shank length.

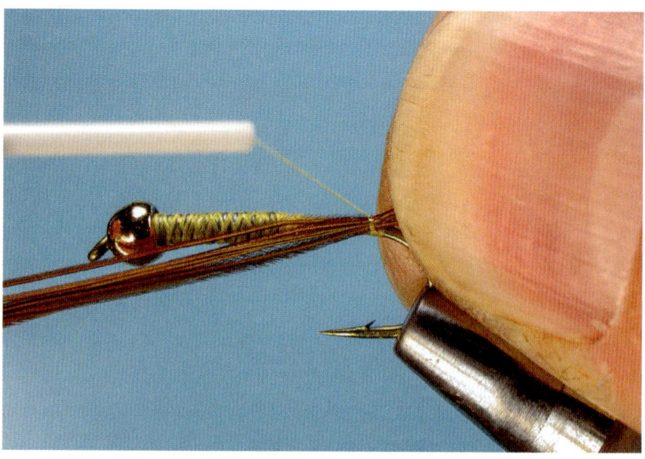

6. Tie the pheasant tail fibers in at the bend of the hook with a few firm wraps.

7. Form a small band of thread anchoring the tail in place at the bend of the hook on top of the shank.

8. Wrap forward over the butt ends of the pheasant tail fibers to just behind the bead. Clip the excess.

9. Clip a length of 3X tippet material and tie it in by holding it across the top of the shank from the far side as shown. The thread torque should roll the end to the far side of the hook, exactly where we want it.

10. Pull the long end of the tippet material down along the far side of the shank as you wrap back over it all the way to the base of the tail. Return thread to the middle of the shank.

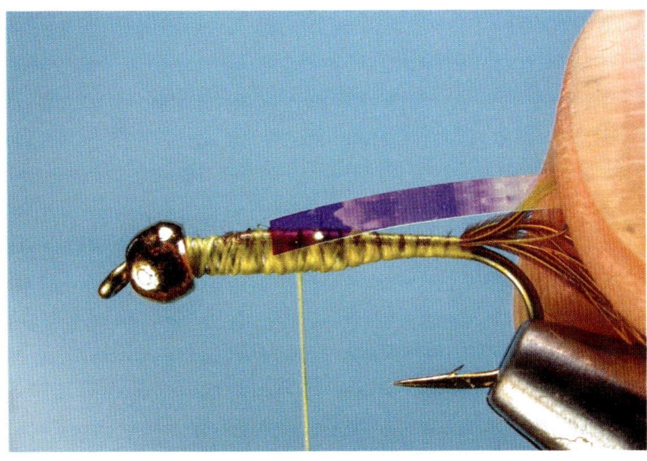

11. Clip a short length of tinsel from the spool and lay it on top of the shank so that it curves down. This will keep it pressed down and out of the way as you tie the rest of the fly rather than curling upward and getting in your way.

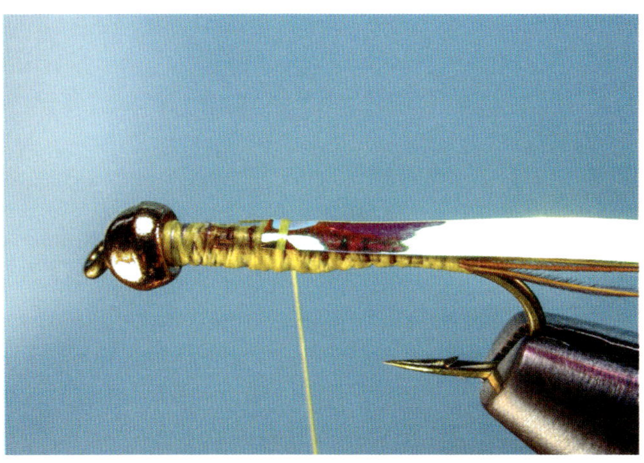

12. Capture the end of the tinsel with a couple turns of thread on top of the lead wraps.

13. Wrap back over the tinsel to the base of the tail, securely lashing the tinsel to the top of the shank.

14. Dub a thin layer of dubbing onto the thread and start the abdomen at the base of the tail. Wrap forward, creating a tapered body as you work up the shank. End the abdomen at about the 75 percent point and leave the bare thread hanging at its front edge.

15. Lift the tinsel up and fold it forward over the abdomen, pulling it ever so slightly toward you so it is just a bit off-center on the near side.

16. Anchor the tinsel down at the front of the abdomen with a few tight turns of thread.

17. Spiral-wrap the tippet material forward through the abdomen and over the tinsel with evenly spaced turns up to the front. The slight cant to the near side should be pulled to top center with the ribbing as you wrap.

18. Tie off the tippet material with several tight wraps of thread and clip the excess.

19. Apply another strand of dubbing to the thread and start building a ball-shaped thorax over the front edge of the abdomen. You can see the stub end of the tinsel sticking out of the front edge of the thorax here, so that should give you a bit of a clue that the thorax actually travels back toward the bend and overlaps the front of the abdomen rather than traveling forward toward the bead.

20. Complete the thorax shape and end with the bare thread hanging at its front edge.

21. Select a medium-sized CDC feather that has nice, full fibers. Strip the fluff from the base of the feather. Preen the fibers back from the tip of the feather to create a separation point on the stem. Do this with the inside curvature of the feather toward the hook shank, just as you would with a more conventional soft-hackle feather. Tie the tip of the feather into the shank just in front of the thorax by capturing the feather at the separation point with several tight turns of thread.

22. Sweep the remaining tip of the feather back along the under, or near, side of the shank and lash it in place with a few more tight wraps. Folding the feather tip here will help keep it from pulling out when we begin to fold and wrap the rest of the feather.

23. You ought to have something that looks like this right now, with the tip of the feather swept under the shank and held in place with a few thread wraps. That square end and stem has to go, so we'll do that next.

24. Reach in with the tips of your scissors and trim the center stem from the tip of the feather, leaving only the loose fibers and no stem. The fish won't care, but I do—and you should too.

25. Grasp the butt end of the feather in your hackle pliers in preparation for folding. Lift the butt end of the feather up with your thread hand; with wetted fingertips, fold the CDC fibers back along the back of the stem. Work the fibers up and down a bit in your fingers to crease them in place.

26. Begin wrapping the folded CDC feather in tight, concentric turns. Make no more than three turns of the feather.

27. Tie the feather off behind the bead with a few firm wraps of thread over the bare feather stem.

28. Clip the butt end of the feather as close as you can and then sweep the CDC fibers back over the body of the fly, making sure they encircle the hook.

29. Make a few turns of thread back along the base of the wrapped CDC feather and over the wound stem to hold the fibers in place and further anchor the stem.

30. Prep a hen saddle feather by clipping the fluff from the base and then trimming the barbs for a short length on either side of the bottom of the feather.

31. Tie the hen feather in by its butt end at the front edge of the CDC collar; the inside of the feather should face the hook. Advance the thread forward to the back of the bead.

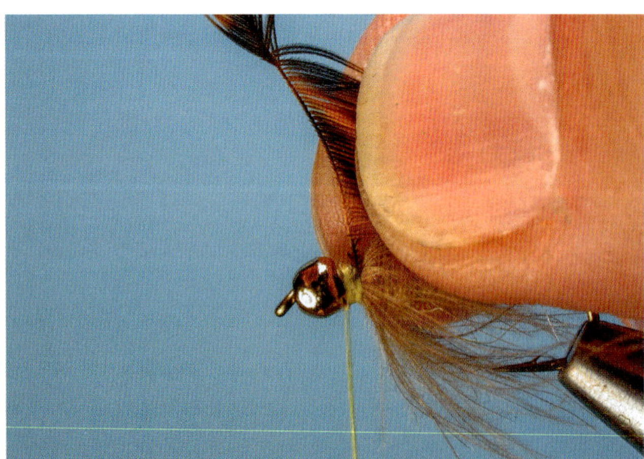

32. Wet your fingers and fold the hen feather as you did with the CDC feather. You don't need a lot of length here; we're only going to make a turn or two.

33. Make at least one, but not more than two, turns with the hen feather, sweeping the fibers back after each turn.

34. Tie off the tip of the hen feather and clip the excess. You should now have a sparse, yet evenly distributed hen collar facing the CDC collar.

35. Anchor the tip of the hen feather with several tight turns of thread behind the bead.

36. Apply a short, thin strand of dubbing to the thread and begin dubbing right behind the bead to cover the tie-down area. This dubbing will just barely cover the front edge of the collar and butt right up to the back of the bead. End with bare thread right behind the bead.

37. Whip-finish on the back edge of the bead and let the wraps slide off the bead into the void at the back, under the dubbed collar.

38. Clip the thread flush. I like to add a drop of head cement to the back of the bead and let it run down onto the thread wraps.

CRANE FLY LARVA

Crane flies are big and ugly and nasty but an important food source for trout. This is an excellent pattern to polish up your tying talents on bulky dubbing, tightly wound ribbing to create defined segmentation, and overall body shaping.

Crane fly larvae are some of the creepiest bugs found on the river bottom and are something you'll never find in a fly-fishing ad. While those spots are reserved for beautiful insects like adult mayflies and occasionally a few flitting caddis bouncing in the sun, the otherwise nasty crane fly larva can indeed become a thing of beauty during conditions you never see in the advertisements. It's the high, dirty water of spring runoff or heavy releases from tailwaters that washes crane flies out of their hidden lairs down in the river bottom and makes them available to the trout.

There is a short "emergence" period in the spring in which some species of crane flies actually burrow into the bank and emerge on land as adults, rather than following the more typical aquatic insect process of hatching into an adult while in the water. Normal flows allow cranes to go about their business tucked safely away well down in the substrate, but higher flows wash them out and make them available to hungry trout. This happens often enough that cranes are a recognized food source for the trout. Robert Younghanz, my resident entomologist buddy, recently explained to me that crane flies can also enter the drift on their own and are thusly available to the trout at any given time of year, and not only during high flows.

Crane fly larvae are found in many trout streams around the country and are way more important than the adults that you might also see flitting on the surface. I typically fish cranes under an indicator, as high water conditions eliminate any chance of using a dry-and-dropper rig or anything more fun than a chunk of yarn or a bobber.

I typically fish cranes under an indicator, as high water conditions eliminate any chance of using a dry-and-dropper rig or anything more fun than a chunk of yarn or a bobber. I tie them heavily to reduce the amount of split shot required, although there are times when a significant amount of additional weight is needed to keep them down along the bottom. I try to concentrate along seam lines and edges when fishing a crane, as these are natural funnels where larger bits of food and flotsam and jetsam collect. The takes can be violent thanks to the combination of hungry fish and swift water colliding at the end of the line, so heavier-than-usual tippet is a good idea. I tie them in sizes 4 through 8, and although there are both larger and smaller versions out there, I find that this range covers my needs.

One of the biggest conundrums in tying large flies with dubbing is getting enough dubbing onto the hook and keeping it tight without making the process cumbersome or lengthy. The direct-dubbing technique I employ here was first shown to me by John Barr well over twenty years ago. John didn't so much demonstrate the technique as simply use it while I was watching, and me being a never-forget-a-fly-tying-tidbit guy, I squirreled it away for later. It has come in handy for dubbing large, thick, shaggy bodies on streamers, leeches, and larger stoneflies as well. You'll have better luck with this technique if you keep the thread between the bobbin and the hook only about as long as your hand is wide and let the dubbing slip from the clump in your palm onto the thread between your fingertips and the hook with each wrap. This results in a thick, shaggy dubbing rope that can be thinned or fattened depending on how much dubbing you allow onto the thread at a time. This method builds large bodies quickly and still allows careful shaping and tapering once you get the hang of it. I love the ragged effect this method gives as well, and a little bit of brushing after the fact yields flies with a beautiful flow. I use this dubbing method on large stonefly nymph patterns, crawdads, streamers and any other larger sized pattern that requires a bulky body.

The rest of this pattern is really pretty straightforward, but like all other "easy" patterns, the devil is in the details. The Thin Skin shellback must be cut wide enough to wrap slightly around the sides of the fly to press the dubbing downward on the finished product. It's easy to cut this strip a bit too narrow. Perhaps the biggest trick in tying this fly is the amount of tension the monofilament ribbing is wrapped with. This pattern's thickly dubbed body and heavy Thin Skin shellback create a firm foundation for the ribbing, and it takes an awful lot of tension on that monofilament to sink it well down into the fly to create adequate body segments. Pull tightly toward you after each turn of ribbing to cinch it down and crease the Thin Skin shell into even segments. This makes for a realistically segmented and buggy pattern and is an easy trick once you get the hang of it.

While crane fly larvae do not have tails, they do have claspers at the rear end of their bodies, represented in the pattern by the short stub of Z-Lon. I have at times skipped this little stub; while the fly works just as well, it seems unfinished to me and I just don't fish it with as much confidence. So for me, the "tail" stays.

CRANE FLY LARVA

Hook: #4-10 TMC 200R
Thread: 3/0 Danville Monocord
Weight: .030- or .025-inch diameter lead wire
Tail: White or light dun Z-Lon
Rib: 3X tippet
Shellback: Tan flyspecks Thin Skin
Body: Smoky olive and tan Wapsi Sow Scud Dubbing

2. Start the thread at the front of the lead wraps and build a small thread dam tapering up to the diameter of the lead itself. Spiral-wrap the thread back over the lead to the bend of the hook. Return the thread to the back of the lead wraps and tie in a whole strand of Z-Lon at the center of its length right at the end of the lead wraps.

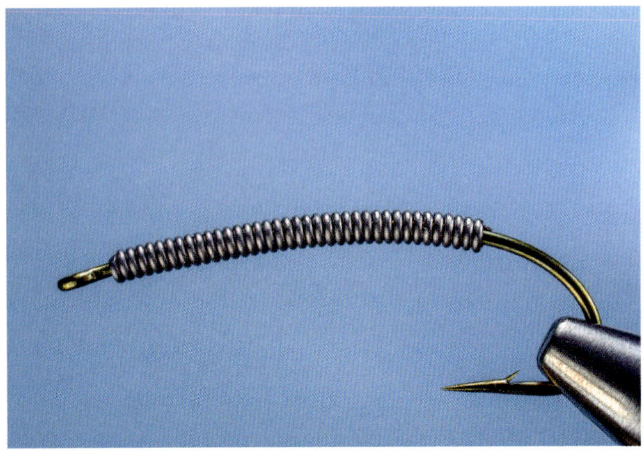

1. Place the hook in the vise and wrap the shank in lead wire up to about an eye length back from the hook eye. I have made about 38 turns of .025-inch diameter lead on this hook and you can see that it pretty well covers the entire shank. You want to make sure to bring the lead up close to the eye to help build the body diameter later, and that you want to leave a bit of room back at the bend to attach the tail without creating a lump. If you want your fly to be lighter in weight, you can use smaller lead wire, but given the high water circumstances when crane flies are most effective, I like to tie mine heavy.

3. Pull the front end of the Z-Lon strand back over the top of the bottom half and bind both ends down tightly to the top of the hook. Wrap back over them down onto the bend of the hook. The bulk of the Z-Lon tie-down should fill in the gap at the back of the lead wraps as shown here.

4. Cut a strip of Thin Skin that is just slightly narrower than the hook gap. Leave the Thin Skin attached to the paper backing and trim one end to a taper (see next step) to help eliminate bulk.

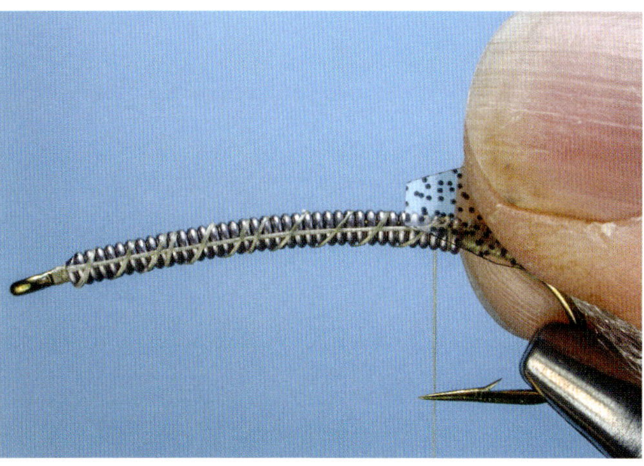

5. Peel the Thin Skin from its paper backing. Tie the material in so that it curves toward the shank. This will keep it out of your way as you tie the rest of the fly.

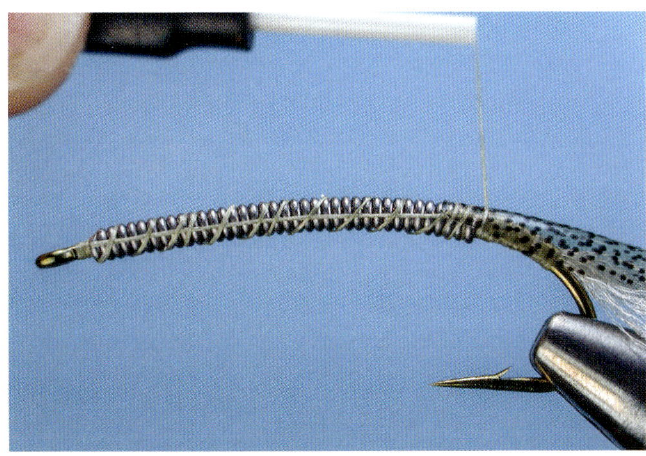

6. Catch the tip of the tapered end with a couple wraps of thread on top of the last of the lead wraps just above the point on the hook.

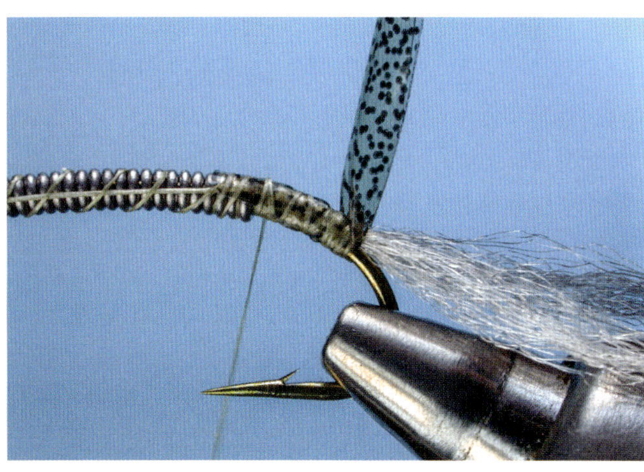

7. Pull the Thin Skin tightly to the bend of the hook so it stretches a bit and buckles down around the hook shank. Wrap tightly back over the Thin Skin to the base of the tail.

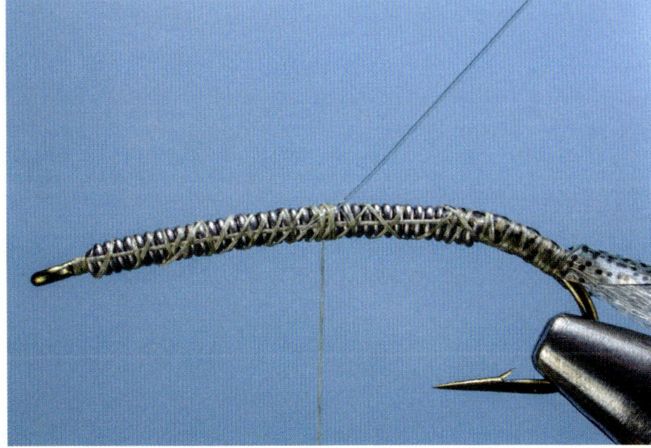

8. Bring the thread to about the midpoint on the shank and tie in a length of 3X tippet material along the near side of the hook. For the time being, you can catch it with a couple turns right in the middle of the hook.

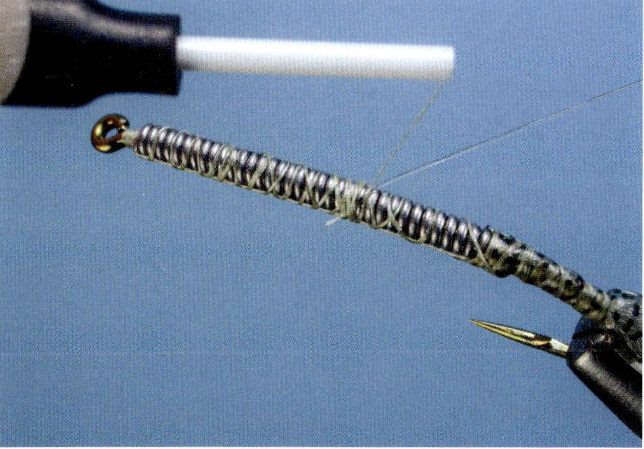

9. Draw the tippet material to the far side of the hook as you wrap back over it, trapping it against the far side of the hook shank.

10. Continue to wrap back over the tippet material all the way to the bend of the hook, keeping it firmly anchored along the far side of the shank.

11. The dubbing technique I like to use on this fly is a bit unconventional and it may help to read through the next several steps before you begin. This technique works well for any long-fibered dubbing and makes it easy to build a large body quickly without the hassle of dubbing three feet of thread. Start by pulling a relatively large clump of dubbing from the bag and loosening the fibers with your fingers; just pull them apart a bit so they are not so tightly compacted. Begin twisting the dubbing from the main clump onto the thread just as you would in a conventional dubbing application.

12. While holding the main dubbing clump in the palm of your hand, begin wrapping the dubbed thread around the hook starting just behind the index point. As you wrap the dubbed thread, hold onto the dubbing clump in the palm of your hand. As you wrap each turn, the clump of dubbing will feed onto and twist around the thread. You can control the amount of dubbing twisting around the thread by varying how far from the hook you hold the clump. Farther away will allow the dubbing to spread out along the thread and make a thinner strand, while holding it closer will allow the dubbing to pile up a little and make for a thicker body.

13. This shows the dubbing twisting around the thread as it's wrapped on the hook. You can see the main clump at the bottom of the photo and how the fibers twist and feed into the thread.

14. As I wrap the dubbing farther back on the shank, I allow the dubbing strand to become thicker by holding it closer to the hook shank and allowing more dubbing to feed into the twist. By drawing the main clump down the thread and farther away, I create a thinner strand of dubbing to wrap toward the bend of the hook to help maintain the body taper. I find it best to draw the dubbing down the thread as you wrap to maintain the twist and feed a slightly smaller amount of dubbing into the rope rather than potentially breaking the strand by pulling down between turns.

15. Wrap the dubbing all the way back to the bend and then forward again to the eye, creating an elongated body that is fattest along its middle. When you approach the hook eye and are almost finished with the dubbed body, remove the main clump of dubbing from the thread and finish up with just what's left attached to the thread. This "direct dubbing" technique makes for a nice shaggy body on large-bodied flies like this and is much faster and easier than conventionally dubbing these patterns.

16. Build a thread base behind the hook eye and leave the thread hanging right in front of the body at the back of the index point.

17. Fold the Thin Skin forward over the top of the fly and pull on it to stretch it slightly. It should buckle around the top of the fly and be centered well. Loop the thread over the Thin Skin behind the hook eye at the front edge of the body. You want this wrap to buckle the Thin Skin down around the shank at the tie-down, so let the Thin Skin support the thread above the hook at the start of the wrap and then pull down on the thread to cinch the Thin Skin around the hook at the front of the body.

18. Try to make this wrap at the back of the index point, thereby leaving yourself a bit of room to later wrap over the stub end cleanly. Anchor the Thin Skin down with three or four tight and stacked wraps of thread. Do not clip the excess Thin Skin yet.

19. Pick up the mono ribbing on the far side of the hook and bring it under the shank and up on the near side. Make sure the mono doesn't lift the edge of the Thin Skin shellback here on this or any other turn as you rib forward.

20. Continue ribbing the mono forward through the body with evenly spaced turns. I like to pull hard on each wrap to sink the mono down into the dubbing and create more prominent segments. Support the hook shank with your fingers as you cinch the mono down tight to keep from disrupting the hook in the vise.

21. Rib the fly all the way up to the index point and then tie off the mono with several tight turns of thread. You can now closely trim the Thin Skin as well as the mono ribbing. We don't trim the Thin Skin until now because wrapping the ribbing actually pulls the Thin Skin shell back tighter and could pull the front end out from under the thread wraps if trimmed prematurely. Trim everything flush and build a smoothly tapered thread head over the butt ends. Whip-finish and clip the thread.

22. Use a strip of the hook side of a piece of Velcro to shag the dubbing out along the bottom and sides of the fly. Don't go too crazy here—cranes have short, stubby legs and we don't want to thin the body out too much with the Velcro.

23. Use the Velcro strip to sweep the loose dubbing down along the bottom of the fly.

24. Pull down on the dubbing and trim it short and straight across along the belly of the fly. This clipped dubbing will better replicate the stubby caterpillar-like legs of the real critter.

25. The trimmed fly should look like this. The clipped dubbing makes a pretty realistic leg impression along the bottom of the fly.

26. Clip the Z-Lon tail to a short stub. Cranes don't have tails per se, but instead they have a clasper at their rear end that this little tuft of Z-Lon represents perfectly.

27. Add a drop of head cement to the thread head. The finished fly should have a smoothly tapered body, similar to an elongated football.

28. Top view. The tightly wound rib provides prominent segmentaion.

CZECH NYMPH

Featuring many of the same techniques as the Crane Fly Larva, the Czech Nymph adds in an ostrich herl thorax and is tied on a smaller hook. You can modify this generic pattern as you wish. The key things to pay attention to here are the weight, overall shape, and deep segmentation of the fly.

Over the past decade or so, European competition-style fishing has gained a strong foothold here in America. Characterized by unusually long leaders, heavy flies, short staccato drifts, and piles of fish in the net, this style of nymphing may not be the most fun way to fish, but the results can't be argued with. I am not a fan of competition in fishing, unless it's between me and a buddy and complete with the requisite smack talk and banter. Official competitions have always taken the fun out of it for me, but that's just my opinion. Luckily, you don't have to be on Team USA to take advantage of some of these unconventional techniques, so consider adding some of the Europeans' more effective methods to your bag of tricks.

While there are many variations on this competition-style fishing (Czech or Spanish, for example) they all seem to revolve around heavily weighted flies that are literally dragged along the bottom of the river, sometimes with

Patterns designed to sink quickly excel in fast pocketwater, especially when fished on a tight line.

a couple smaller and lighter buddies. A few years ago I spent a day on Colorado's Big Thompson River with Riley Cotter, a member of Team USA and an incredibly voracious fish-catching machine. I'm confident enough to say I'm no slouch in the fish-catching department and thought it was mighty noble of old Riley to let me fish my dry-and-dropper rig through all the best-looking water first. I remember working my way through a run—catching several fish—and then watching Riley set up on the other side of the river. Wondering how long he'd fish through burned-up water, I started upstream in pursuit of a few more trout. I didn't make it more than a few steps before Riley had a fish on. Then he had another. And then another. Riley went through that run in short order—casting his rig, leading it downstream, and then setting the hook on every cast—all the while catching an obscene number of fish.

While Riley's method was unconventional, his hooking a fish on nearly every cast certainly got my attention. I finally just planted my butt on the bank and watched him hoover fish out of the river, from water I had just fished and *waded* through! There was no arguing with his success, and while reading the water seemed to go out the window (he simply covered *all* of it) and the beauty and grace of the cast was nonexistent, he was more often than not wrenching a flopping trout from the water into his giant net. It really was a spectacle to watch.

When I later tried the technique for myself, I found out that it's really not too hard to pick up. It reminded me of drifting a worm and a split shot on a spinning rod as a kid, and the familiar tap-tap-tap of the shot bouncing on the bottom with the youthful rig was replaced with the same feeling of the heavy flies ticking the rocks. The long, thin leaders favored by the experts cut through the water easily and don't drag while telegraphing the slightest tick into the rod tip.

It's this hypersensitive connection between the flies and the rod tip that makes this such an effective technique. The combination of the long leader coming out of the tip-top of the rod (any fly line in the tip deadens the sensitivity) and going straight down to the flies under slight tension creates a direct conduit from river bottom to rod hand and instantly alerts the angler to any hesitation or anomalies in the drift. I found that with even a little bit of practice, not only could I detect the strikes immediately, but in many cases could tell if it was a fish of decent size or a tiddler . . . it's *that* sensitive!

As far as what are now conventionally known as Czech

Nymph patterns, the fly I present here is just a generic representative sample. Usually tied to resemble caddis larvae, Czech Nymphs typically feature a shellback and ribbing over a dubbed body, with or without a hot spot of brightly colored dubbing placed somewhere from the midpoint forward. The color combinations are endless and there are certainly other little proprietary tidbits that each tier likes to add to his or her own version, but the most common denominator is that the flies are generally tied quite heavy. (Angling savant George Daniel points out that patterns tied specifically for slower water or for fishing the middle to upper water column may not be quite so heavily weighted.)

Weighted with lead wire and sometimes a tungsten bead or three, the weight keeps these flies down along the bottom, right in the fish's face, as well as tethered tightly to the end of a taut tippet, which makes detecting strikes much easier. There are a variety of "competition hooks" available that are readily appropriate for a fly like this. As the rules of the game prohibit barbed hooks, all competition hooks are barbless and many of them feature an elongated point and spear to help keep the fish pinned. Of course, if you're not fishing in a competition, you are welcome to use any hook you like.

I'm not sure I am convinced that every fish actually *eats* the fly though. I had a sneaking suspicion that dragging the fly right along the bottom tethered to a taut line drags the fly into the fish's mouth more often than we'd like to admit, but then a dear friend of mine (who's also a good angler) politely brought up the point that Czech nymphing simply covers the water where the fish are so much more effectively that it keeps you fishing where the fish are a much higher percentage of the time. When I think about it that way, I may just have to agree. When you consider that on a conventional indicator-rig drift, the fly has to sink to the bottom and then drift a few feet before it starts to rise up as the line tightens, the resulting amount of actual useable drift along the key fish habitat (dead on the bottom of the river) is a lot less than we are prone to think.

The Czech nymphing technique does indeed keep the fly right where it needs to be for a longer period of time; coupled with a much more sensitive rig, it's the equivalent of carpet bombing the river bottom with tasty trout morsels. It ain't the prettiest way to fish and I don't *love* it (other than the catching lots of fish part, anyway). For me, real casting is an inherent part of fly fishing and I enjoy it too much to really get into this type of fishing, although I have to admit that it was certainly fun to learn (another inherent part of fly fishing—never get too smart to learn something new) and add the technique to my bag of tricks.

George Daniel slips a pair of nymphs into a pocket upstream of a boulder on Pennsylvania's Big Spring Creek. Tight line nymphing allows for very precise drifts where your flies are almost immediately in the fishes' zone.

NET BUILDER/CZECH NYMPH

Hook: #8-14 Umpqua C300BL
Weight: .015- or .020-inch diameter lead or nonlead wire
Thread: Black 8/0 Uni
Clasper: Dun Z-Lon
Shellback: Olive flyspecks Thin Skin
Rib: 3X tippet material
Body: Caddis green Nature's Spirit Emergence Dubbing
Legs: Black ostrich herl

NET-BUILDER CADDIS

Hook: #8-14 Umpqua C300BL
Bead: Black tungsten
Weight: Lead wire
Thread: Black 8/0 Uni
Clasper: Dun Z-Lon
Shellback: Olive flyspecks Thin Skin
Rib: 3X tippet material
Body: Olive Nature's Spirit Emergence Dubbing
Legs: Black ostrich herl

The bead head version allows the opportunity to add even more weight, particularly when tungsten beads are employed. Faster, deeper runs require heavier flies and having a few variations with and without beads and in a variety of weights will help you cover all depths and speeds when fishing.

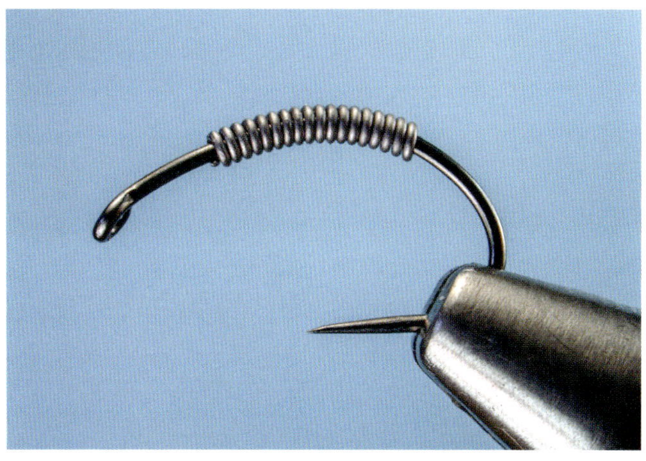

1. Depending on how heavy you want your fly, make up to 18 wraps of lead wire around the shank, keeping them centered on the hump.

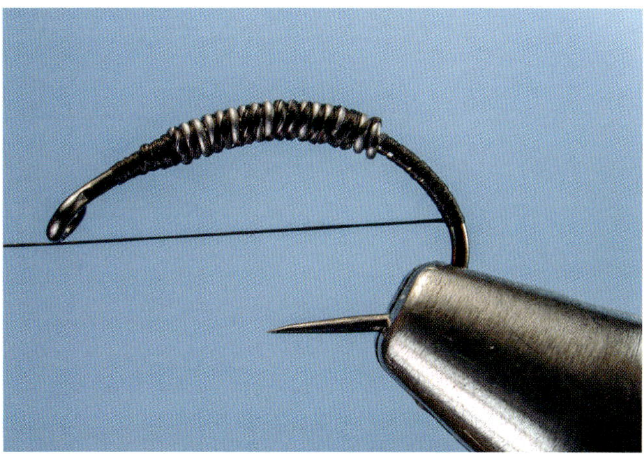

2. Start the thread about an eye length back from the hook eye and build a small thread dam from the bare shank up to the lead. Wrap back over the lead and back down onto the shank behind it. Keep wrapping on the hook bend until you can draw the thread forward and make a straight line to the bottom of the hook eye. This is a good rule of thumb for where to stop the body on any fly tied on a curved hook shank. Return the thread to the midpoint on the shank.

3. Divide a clump of dun Z-Lon (or as appropriate for the hook size) and lay it on top of the shank.

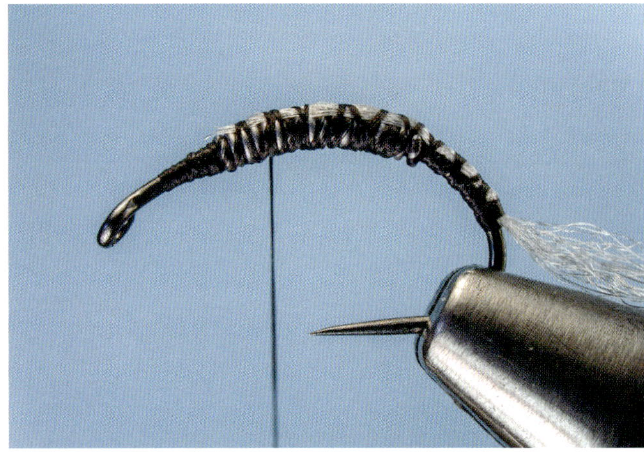

4. Catch the end of the Z-Lon at midshank and pull it down flush to the thread wraps. Wrap back over the Z-Lon to the end of the thread base, hereafter known as "the bend." Return the thread to the tie-in point, taking care to keep things smooth as you go.

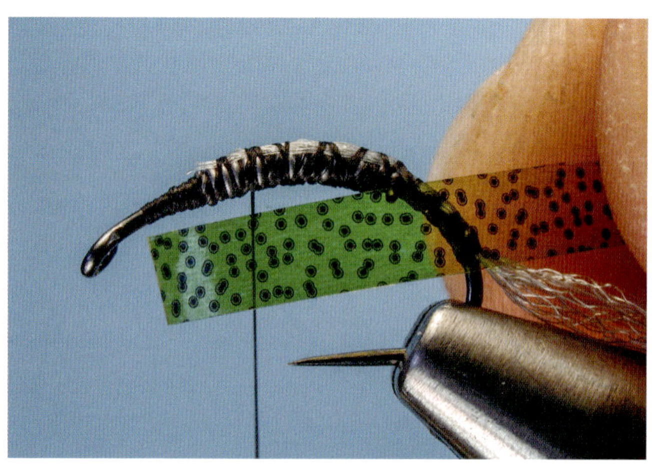

5. Cut a strip of Thin Skin and remove the paper backing. The Thin Skin strip should be about half as wide as the hook gap. This hook has a really wide gap, so we have to think about that for this shellback. If you're using a different hook you may have to use some trial and error.

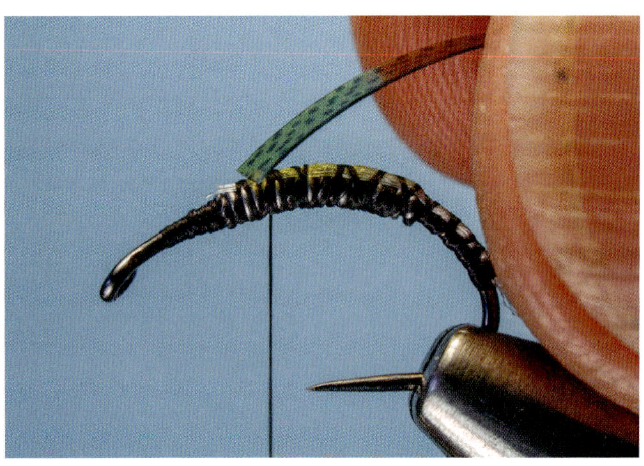

6. The Thin Skin will have a curve to it once it is removed from the paper backing. Lay the Thin Skin on top of the shank at the center of the hook with the curve down.

7. Press the end of the Thin Skin down on top of the hook with your thumb. This will hold it flat against the hook as you catch it with a wrap of thread.

8. Catch the end of the Thin Skin with a couple wraps of thread, making sure to buckle the Thin Skin downward around the shank so it cups to the hook.

9. Pull down on the thread to keep the wraps tight and pull firmly back on the Thin Skin toward the bend of the hook. The Thin Skin will stretch a bit and curl around the hook, which will make the next step a whole lot easier. Keep pulling on the Thin Skin as you wrap back over it to the bend (remember that time we decided, together, that we were gonna call the base of the tail "the bend"?). Keep the Thin Skin buckled down around the shank as you wrap over it.

10. Return the thread to the tie-in point and catch the end of a piece of 3X tippet material. Try to let the thread roll it to the far side of the shank, but if not, catch it where you can and then pull it to the far side and anchor it in place there.

11. Hold the tippet material along the far side of the shank as you wrap back over it to the bend, then return the thread to the starting point.

12. Apply a strand of coarse dubbing to the thread and work back so the first turn of dubbing comes around the shank at the bend of the hook. I still like to keep this strand thin, even on larger flies, as I can keep thin dubbing tighter on the thread and it gives me a bit more ability to control the shape and taper of the body.

13. Dub all the way forward up to the index point, forming a slightly humped body shape that is fattest in the middle and tapers down at both ends. The body should only have a slight swell at its middle, not a big lump.

14. Spiral-wrap the thread back over the front edge of the dubbed body at the 75–80 percent point. Strip the end of a bushy ostrich herl, leaving an exposed bare stem.

15. Anchor the stem in place at the 75 to 80 percent point with several tight turns of thread over the dubbing. Return the thread to the hook eye.

16. Spiral-wrap the herl forward over the dubbing with about five turns to the hook eye. Tie off the ostrich at the eye and clip the excess.

17. Wet your fingers a little bit and stroke the ostrich herl down and to the sides of the fly. If you wet the ostrich down a bit it should stay in place for the moment.

18. Pull the Thin Skin tightly forward over the top of the fly, taking great pains to keep it centered on top of the hook shank. Your ribbing material will want to stick out to the far side when you do this, and that's fine—just don't let it get in your way.

19. Catch the front of the Thin Skin behind the hook eye with a couple of firm thread wraps. Do not cut the Thin Skin yet. Make sure the Thin Skin is centered on the top of the fly; if it's not, push, slide, or otherwise cajole it with your fingertip to where it needs to be.

20. Pick up the tippet material and begin to spiral-wrap it forward over the back end of the body with evenly spaced turns. Pull hard on these wraps to sink the tippet material down into the Thin Skin and dubbing. Wrap right up to the back of the ostrich herl and wait there for a second.

21. Take a wide wrap under the shank with the tippet material and divide the ostrich herl section in half as you come over the top. Again, pull tightly to make these sections apparent.

22. Make one more tight turn of tippet material, dividing the last segment of ostrich in half again. Come up from the bottom of the hook and end at the hook eye. Catch the tippet material with several firm wraps of thread at the hook eye.

23. Clip the excess Thin Skin as well as the tippet material flush behind the hook eye. Build a smooth thread head to cover the stubs cleanly and then whip-finish.

24. Use a black Sharpie to color the tops of the last three segments at the front of the body to imitate the thoracic segments.

25. Add a drop of head cement to the thread wraps and clip the Z-Lon claspers into a short brush.

6

DITCH DAMSEL

Jay Zimmerman's Ditch Damsel is one of the most creative interpretations I have seen for this ubiquitous stillwater insect. The design elements on the wing and wire body ensure the fly rides hook point up and the use of dyed mallard flank adds a slight bit of variegation to the pattern.

Damselfly nymphs inhabit lakes, ponds, and slow-moving rivers. They are most active in the late spring and early summer. They emerge on dry land, and as such, their pre-emergence is marked by a mass exodus toward the bank, where the nymphs can crawl out onto a sun-laden stick and dry their exoskeletons before hatching into the wonderful and acrobatic flying blue darts we see in the thrushes. Damselfly nymphs are long, skinny critters with big eyes, and they slide and swim with a seductive side-to-side action as they migrate toward dry ground. Trout, bass, and panfish all have a taste for these slender bites, and when you're in the right place at the right time, the action can be crazy.

Damsel patterns need to be tied slim and sparse, with a bit of weight to keep them swimming shallow and with as much wiggle and shimmy as one can manage. This is a tall order from a fly-designing standpoint. Luckily for me and you, I just happen to work with Jay Zimmerman, one of the most creative fly designers any of us will ever meet. He and I often take a minute at the shop first thing in the morning to discuss what we tied the night before,

A good damsel imitation is essential on most stillwater fisheries. Trout, bass, and panfish all have a taste for these slender bites, and when you're in the right place at the right time, the action can be crazy.

or to share theories and ideas on new patterns. It was in one of these little brainstorming sessions that Jay first revealed this pattern to me. It immediately caught my eye, not only from a creative standpoint, but also from Jay's seamless melding and blending of materials to reach an end.

The Ditch Damsel, as Jay calls his fly, is clearly a product of his wonderfully creative and sometimes scattered brain. His damsel nymph pattern achieves the highly sought-after combination of being truly unique and unconventional while still being perfectly practical and easy to tie. There aren't many patterns that strike me as completely unique these days, and I knew the moment I saw Jay's creation that it was going to be a hit. Every single material on this fly is used and applied in a distinctive and thoughtful way, and they combine to create a wonderful profile and shape. The fact that Jay went so totally out of the box to create it makes it even more appealing to me. I get so excited about stuff like this at this point in my life and I am not embarrassed to say I really wish I would have come up with this one myself.

Tied on a long shank hook in the inverted position, the fly swims hook point-up and relatively snag-free. The ingenious use of a two-toned wire body to counterweight the hook and achieve this point-up attitude in the water while still being accurately slim and beautiful is one of those things that a fly designer looks at and smacks his head. Though this technique is well used in other tying arenas, applying it to a small and thin damsel nymph is pure brilliance. Jay uses a marabou wing to further help the inversion, as well to give the fly a slinky action on the water. Not leaving well enough alone, Jay also adds a few strands of finely barred dyed mallard or wood duck fibers to the flank of the wings to create a bit of mottling and variegation as well as a heaping teaspoon of class.

Perhaps the most underappreciated and trailblazing technique he used here was stacking a small clump of rabbit fur on the top of the front of the wing. While the fly is dry, this clump just seems to blend into the wing and may leave you wondering why it's even there, but when wet, this clump melds into the wing, creating an ever-so-slightly thicker thorax to accurately mimic the real thing. Finished off with a pair of wriggling Sili Legs and melted mono eyes, this fly is a dead ringer for the real thing and is easily cast, won't foul or snag up, and is completely different than anything we've seen before. Simple, common materials blended together smartly to create a unique look and a practical fly—man, I love this stuff! The fact that this fly can cross over well and imitate a leech makes it a great searching pattern for both cold- and warmwater fish during the warmer months.

DITCH DAMSEL

Hook: #10-14 TMC 200R
Thread: Yellow olive 70-denier UTC
Tag: Opal Mirage Tinsel (medium)
Body: Olive and silver UTC Wire (small)
Eyes: Melted 16-pound-test hard mono, colored black
Wing: Golden-olive marabou
Sides: Mallard flank dyed wood duck gold
Thorax: Olive rabbit fur
Legs: Olive-barred nymph Sili Legs
Head: Dragonfly olive SLF Dave Whitlock Dubbing

1. Start the thread right behind the hook eye and wrap a smooth and flat thread base from there to just slightly down onto the hook bend.

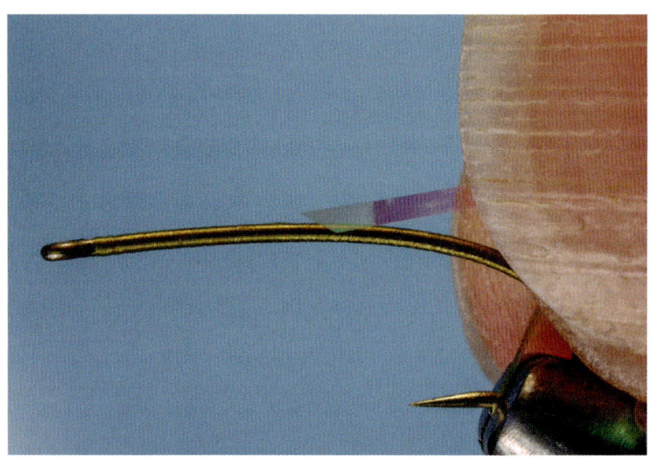

2. Cut the end of the Mirage Tinsel at a long angle, leaving a pointed tip.

3. Catch the tip end of the Mirage Tinsel under a couple flat wraps of thread at the end of the thread base.

4. Return the thread to the hook eye, keeping it flat on the hook as you go. This may require you to stop and unwind the thread a bit, so don't be afraid to do that.

5. Wrap the Mirage Tinsel forward with abutting turns all the way to the hook eye. Again, make sure to keep these wraps as flat and smooth as possible. Tie the tinsel off at the eye of the hook and clip the excess.

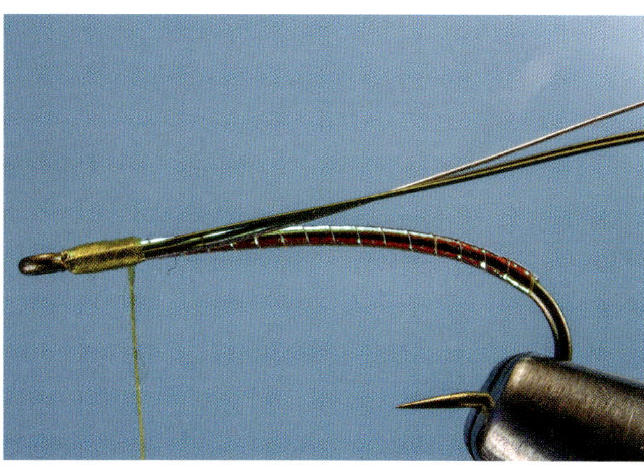

6. Break two strands of olive and one strand of silver wire from the spool. You need to even up the ends; you'll be tempted to clip them even with your scissors, but rather than ruin the scissor tips, use your thumbnail to butt the ends up and square them that way. Catch the end of all three strands of wire under a narrow band of thread right behind the hook eye. Pull the butt ends of the wire down to length so they are just behind the eye.

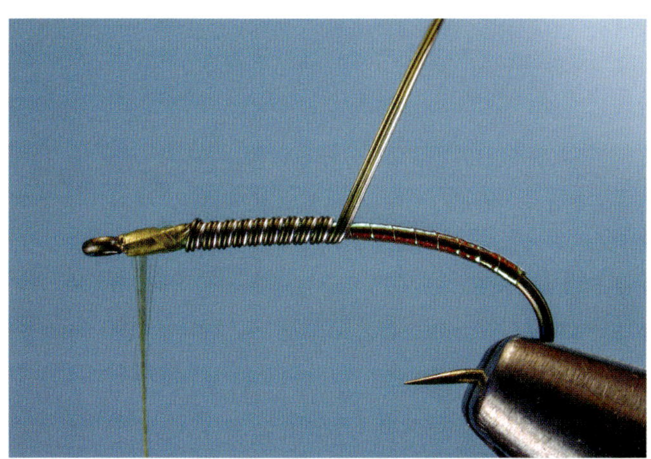

7. Begin wrapping all three strands of wire, as one unit, back toward the bend of the hook in tight, abutting turns.

8. Continue wrapping the wire back to a point just above the hook barb (this particular hook just so happens to be a barbless model, but I have a good imagination and know where the barb would be). Once you reach the bend, you should have a short tag of Mirage Tinsel sticking out past the end of the wire body. You want to leave this exposed to add a little sparkle and flash. Grasp the ends of all three wire strands close to the hook and helicopter (twist around in a circle like a helicopter blade) the wire until it breaks off flush.

9. The body ought to look a lot like this.

10. Invert the hook in the vise. Be careful not to pinch the tinsel tag in the jaws of the vise here.

11. Place a set of melted mono eyes on what is now the top of the hook about an eye length back from the hook eye. Make three or four turns of thread from the back of the eyes on the near side to the front of the eyes on the far side, forming the first leg of an X wrap. Make three or four more wraps in the opposite direction, from the near front to far back side of the eyes to square them up on the hook. Repeat the process one more time to anchor the eyes firmly in place.

12. Select a straight marabou feather with a square tip. Clip the tip out of the feather and wet it a bit to tame the fibers down. Measure the marabou feather against the hook so it extends from just behind the eyes to about a shank length beyond the hook bend.

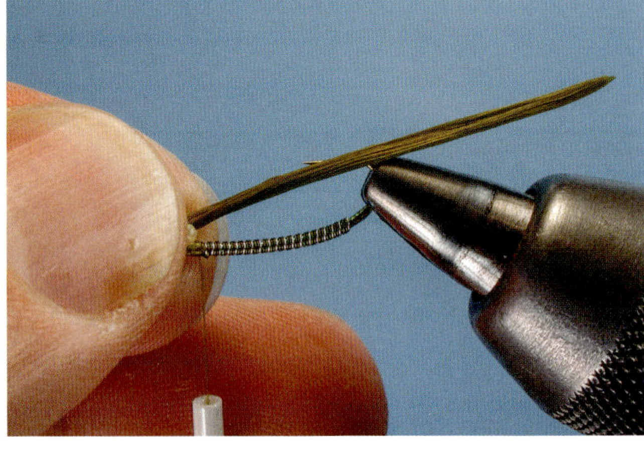

13. Run the tip of the marabou feather through your mouth to wet it well. Don't be squeamish about it—you won't get cooties and this will make mounting the wing much easier. Measure the wetted feather once more. Hold the feather in place just behind the eyes with your thread hand.

14. Reach in and transfer the marabou feather to your material hand. Be careful of the upward-pointing hook point here—damsels with blood on them aren't realistic. Pinch the base of the marabou feather down behind the eyes.

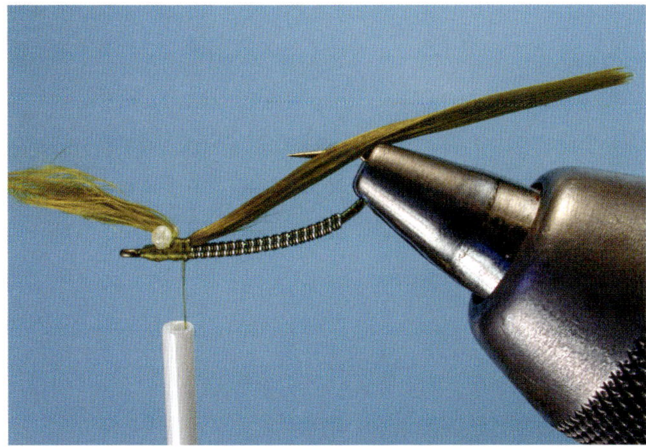

15. Catch the base of the marabou feather with a couple turns of thread to anchor it squarely on top (really the bottom) of the hook.

16. Select a well-marked dyed gold mallard flank feather and preen out four or six fibers so their tips are even.

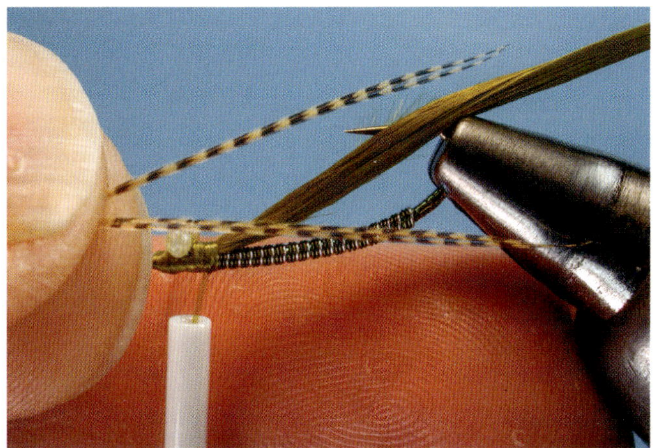

17. Peel the fibers from the stem and divide them slightly in the fingertips of your thread hand. Lay the mallard fibers up against the hook so the tips reach about two-thirds of the way up the wing and there is one bunch of two or three fibers on each side of the hook point.

18. Pinch the mallard fibers down right behind the eyes on either side of the wing and hook point using your material hand.

19. Take two wraps over the mallard fibers to bind them in place. Don't sweat it if they don't line up with the marabou wing perfectly yet; they will when the fly gets wet.

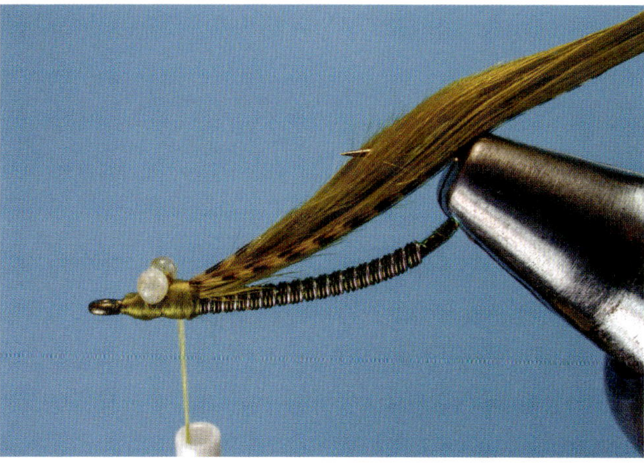

20. Clip the butt ends of the mallard fibers off flush at the eyes.

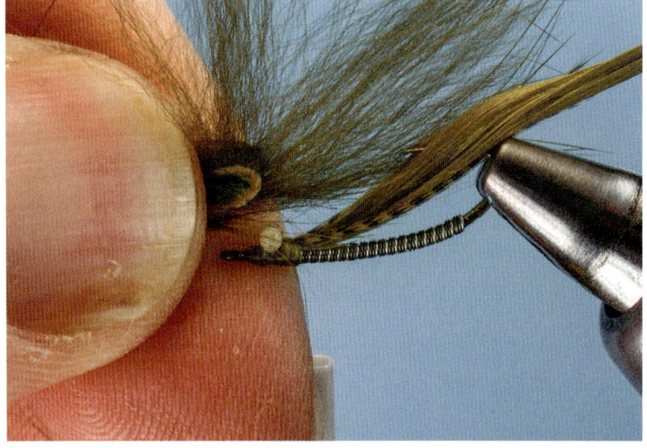

21. Fold the end of an olive rabbit strip, fanning the fur out from the hide. You want a pretty sparse bunch of fur here and you can easily separate out a small clump by folding the hide like this. Grasp the fur tightly in your fingertips and rip it straight out of the hide.

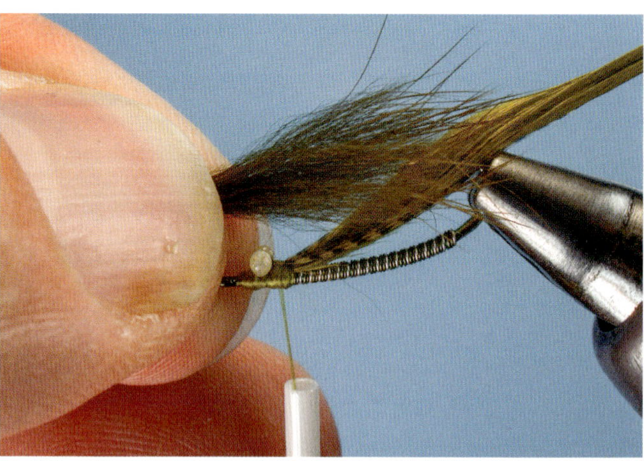

22. Measure the clump of rabbit fur against the marabou wing so it is about half as long as the wing itself.

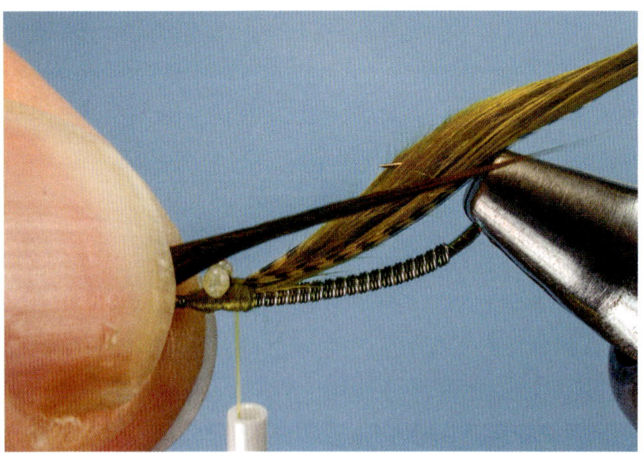

23. Wet the rabbit fur clump so it slicks down a bit and is easier to handle.

24. Pinch the rabbit fur down behind the eyes exactly as you did with the marabou and mallard fibers. Make a few thread wraps over the base of the rabbit behind the eyes. Clip the excess butt ends flush.

25. The rabbit should reach just past the bend of the hook. Again, watch out for the upturned point here. Trim the butt ends of the rabbit fur flush behind the eyes.

26. Loop a length of olive-barred Sili Legs around the shank between the hook eye and the mono eyes.

27. Catch the Sili Legs with just a couple wraps of thread behind the eyes at the base of the wing. These first two wraps will hold the legs in place while you pull down on each side in turn to square them up along the *sides* of the fly. Once the legs are positioned, cinch them in place with a couple more tight thread turns.

28. The legs should be along the sides of the fly as shown here, not on top of the wing. Dub the thread with what will seem like a ridiculously small amount of dubbing. You want a thin strand as we have a bit of a travel to make here and we don't want to bulk the head up too much. Think of tying a size 20 midge when you apply this dubbing to the thread. Most of the bulk needed to fill out the head is already there in the form of all the thread wraps we have made; the dubbing is going to add texture and color, but little bulk.

29. Before you wrap the dubbing, color the eyes with a black Sharpie. Make sure to get all the way around them. I leave the coloring of the eyes until now so I don't rub the ink off in the previous tying steps. From this point forward, avoid touching the eyes. Once they dry they'll be fine. Truth be told, damsel nymph eyes are really closer to the color of the plain mono than black, but black makes the fly look way sexier.

30. Grab the marabou wing, the rabbit tuft, and the legs in your thread hand and pull them up and forward over the hook eye. Make three or four turns of dubbing up against the base of the wing (behind it) to prop everything up a bit.

31. Continue dubbing forward to the back of the mono eyes.

32. Make a couple of X-wraps with the dubbed thread through the eyes, forming a rounded head. Finish up with a single turn of dubbing around the hook in front of the eyes and end with bare thread right behind the hook eye.

33. Whip-finish and clip the tying thread. Trim the legs even with the back end of the wire body.

34. The fly when wet. An optional step recommended by the designer is to apply a thin coat of Sally Hansen Hard As Nails to the wire body.

Lisa Mitchell lifts a nice rainbow she caught sight fishing with a damsel pattern. Being in the right place at the right time is the secret to big fish, and big smiles.

7

MCFLY FOAM EGG

Egg flies are the hard working but ugly cousins to real trout flies. An incredibly viable food source, eggs are tremendously effective but can be tough to tie well. Paying close attention to technique and choosing the right materials will help you achieve perfection.

Over the past several years, I have had the wonderful opportunity to do fly-tying demos not just all over my home state of Colorado, but all over the country. I love sharing skills with a crowd and often try to highlight some of my signature patterns and techniques in hopes of wowing the spectators. At some point in the evening, I usually ask if there's anything that anyone just has to see—some fly or technique they have trouble with that I might be able to shine a little light on. It has amazed me the amount of times that the requested fly or technique has been not a spun deer hair fly or intricate parachute hackle wrapping technique, but instead a simple egg pattern!

Now, I don't mean to say that everyone shouts out, "Tie an egg, Charlie! Please, please, Charlie, tie an egg for us!" It's never like that. It's some quiet guy a few rows back who shields his mouth with his hand and, trying to cast his voice from another room, meekly says, "Can you tie an egg?" Then another guys softly pipes in with a "Yeah, an egg would be good . . . I'd watch that." I always comply because, well, *I've been there* and by the time I dig the materials out the whole room is silent and at rapt attention. No one wants to admit they have trouble with (a) tying a simple egg pattern and (b) admitting that they fish them, but when the opportunity arises to see how they're really tied and all the tips and techniques that go into making them perfectly round, well . . . let's just say I have the audience right where I want them.

All kidding aside, egg flies are tricky to tie. I have used a variety of techniques over the years with varying degrees of success before finally settling on the method I'll share here. Material selection is of the utmost importance, even though there are really only two materials: gel-spun polyethylene (GSP) thread and McFly Foam yarn.

GSP thread is superstrong, thin, and slippery, which allows me to not only tightly bind the material to the shank with almost no thread bulk, but its inherent slickness lets it slide around the material and keeps it from bunching up. It is the only thread I'll use for eggs and it comes in a few sizes, although I try to use the thinnest thread possible. The color of the thread is of no importance, as the thread doesn't show on the finished fly, but I typically use white thread for any color egg just to keep things simple.

I am well aware of, and familiar with, the conventional egg yarn products that have been available for years, but I find that the elasticity and compressibility of McFly Foam are key to getting a nice and round finished product. Using these two carefully selected materials is seven-eighths of the battle in making a perfect egg—the rest is easy.

The actual technique needed to tie an egg properly is tricky because everyone tries to overcomplicate it. If you can tie a pair of lead eyes to a hook or tie a set of spent wings, you are already well versed in the best way to tie an egg. Simple X-wraps lash the McFly Foam to the hook cleanly with little bulk and create an inconspicuous tie-down that remains well hidden on the finished fly. Tying

Trout everywhere love eggs. Tie them in different sizes and colors to match both local fare and water conditions.

the yarn perpendicular to the hook gives you a much better chance at getting a round egg, as you are creating a half sphere on each side of the hook that then flares around and meets the other half in the middle, forming a perfectly round ball.

I don't suppose now is a great time to tell you that eggs don't really have to be round to catch fish, is it? Trout eat the eggs of other trout and salmon, even their very own in some cases, for two reasons: An egg is an easily captured, high-protein food source and eating one eliminates further competition. It seems to me if the fly is tied in some shade of orange and fished at the right time of year, it can border on unsporting. There, I said it. I didn't say I haven't done it or that I won't do it again, but let's not kid ourselves—there's a reason so many otherwise uncatchable fish fall to egg imitations every year and it's not because we all suddenly became much better anglers. The poor things are just genetically wired to gobble up eggs, and some of the wildest experiences I've had out on the water have proven this:

I have seen wild brown trout swim up and eat an egg fly that is snagged on the bottom.

I've seen trout eat an egg pattern, get hooked, run, jump, spit the hook, and then circle back and eat it again!

I've seen them stare at it, run away, come back, and stare some more before finally giving in to the impulse and snatching it up off the bottom.

I've seen them chase down a drifting egg fly that's dragging like a speedboat, and not care one bit about the drift.

There have been countless other embarrassingly undignified instances where otherwise wild, wary, and crafty fish have turned into silly, starved stockers, all because of the appearance of a stray egg in their field of vision.

This is not to say that pressured fish won't or don't get wise to egg flies and demand increasingly more realistic imitations and perfect drifts. They can and do. Half the fun of fishing is developing your own theories and patterns and tweaking them and making adjustments, even if they are really only in your head. I'm not passing judgment here, just sharing my limited experiences. And yes, I carry a box of eggs in my pack . . . you know, just in case.

MCFLY FOAM EGG

Hook: #10-18 TMC 2488H
Thread: White 50-denier GSP
Egg: McCheese and Golden McFly Foam

NUKE EGG

Hook: #10-18 TMC 2457 or 2488H
Thread: White 50-denier GSP, head colored with Sharpie
Egg: McFly Foam
Veil: White egg yarn

1. Start the GSP thread right behind the eye and make a thread base back to about midway between the point on the hook and the barb. Then return forward to the eye and end with the thread hanging in the center of this thread base just in front of the hook point. Make sure this thread base is firmly anchored to the shank; this thread is slippery and requires a tight base to adhere properly to the hook shank. It's also hard to cut unless it's under tension.

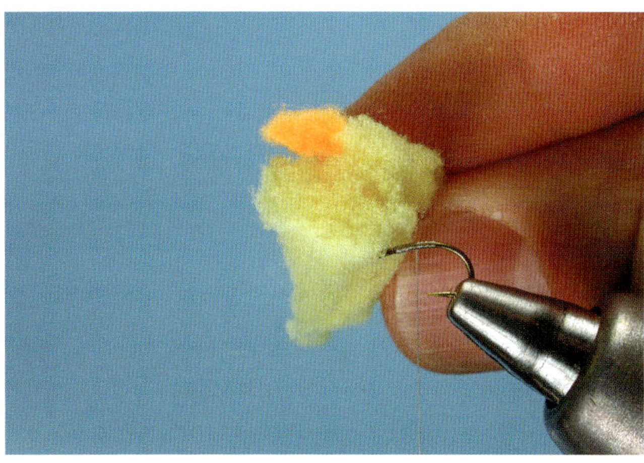

2. Peel a clump of your primary color McFly Foam from the bunch. You want more than you think you'll need, but don't get crazy with it. For a size 14 egg, the clump I'm using is about as big around as the tip of my index finger. Peel a much smaller strand of McFly Foam in a contrasting color and lay this strand on top of the main clump to form the yolk. This step is optional, but as long as I'm showing you, I may as well give you the whole enchilada. The clump only needs to be about three inches long, and the shorter the better because there is a lot of inherent waste in egg patterns.

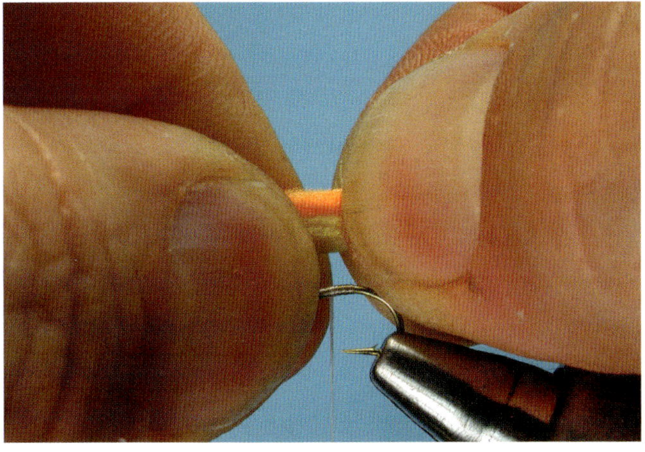

3. Pull the center of the clump of McFly Foam down tight between your fingertips, compressing it as tightly as you can.

4. Lay the clump on the top of the hook shank with the compressed portion pinched in your fingertips just behind the hanging thread.

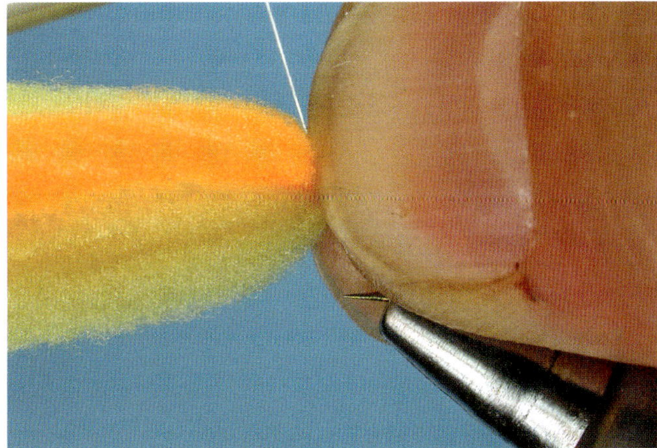

5. Bring the thread up and over the McFly Foam, placing one tight turn and then another, one on top of the other.

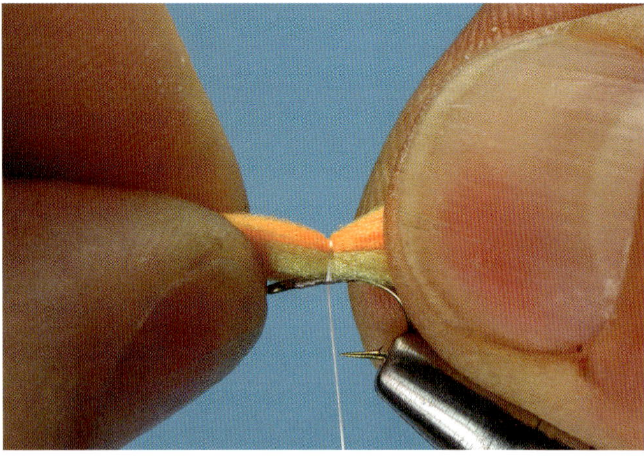

6. These two turns should be stacked on top of each other and not at all spread out horizontally. Pull on the ends of the yarn to compress the bunch further and let the wraps stack up neatly. Pull down on the thread to cinch the wraps tight.

7. Pull the back end of the McFly Foam clump so it faces away from you on the far side of the hook; then bring the front end toward you on the near side. When you pull both ends tightly the thread should magically form a diagonal across the hook shank. This is the first half of the X-wraps we will use to anchor the material.

8. Let go of the ends of the material and make two more wraps going diagonal across the McFly Foam from front to back. You can use your free hand to pull on the far end of the material to open up your view to the shank to help make sure these wraps are stacked atop each other as the first two were.

9. Pull both ends down as tightly as you can to expose what should be a tightly stacked X of thread anchoring the material cleanly to the hook. You don't want these wraps spread out at all, just neatly stacked and forming a tight, perfect X.

10. Pull both ends of the material to the rear of the hook, bring the thread to just behind the eye, and whip-finish. You'll need to hold the McFly Foam taut to keep it out of the way. Clip the thread.

11. Pull all the McFly Foam tightly above the hook and compress it as much as possible. Pull the material straight up, but don't twist it at all.

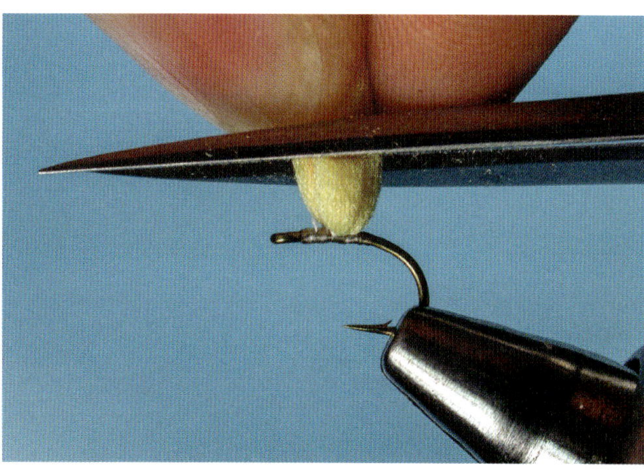

12. While holding the material tightly upright, come in with your sharpest scissors and make a single, straight cut across the McFly Foam.

13. If you do this right, once you make the one clean cut, you'll have a perfectly round little egg. The farther you make this cut from the shank, the bigger and looser the egg will be. If you want a big, dense egg, you'll need to use more McFly Foam; if you want a small, dense egg, you can cut a bit closer to the shank. I like them just a bit smaller than a garden pea.

14. The yolk shows up on top, and although optional, adds a bit of panache to an otherwise boring "fly."

8

GILLED NYMPH

The Gilled Nymph is a bit out of the box when compared to many mayfly nymph patterns. Mastering the ostrich herl abdomen and melding it into the thorax area cleanly are both fine points that often make tiers stumble.

All mayfly nymphs have gills, so it may seem a bit redundant that this Shane Stalcup pattern goes by the name Gilled Nymph. Mayfly nymph species that inhabit slow or still water fall under the heading of swimmers, and because there is less dissolved oxygen in still water, their gills are larger and more obvious than those on their swift-water brethren. *Siphlonurus* and *Callibaetis* are two prominent still- and slow-water species that anglers encounter on a fairly regular basis. The Gilled Nymph pattern tied here is representative of a *Callibaetis* mayfly nymph, and the size and color can be adjusted to match other species as well as variations among the species.

This pattern is hugely popular on Colorado reservoirs during the summerlong *Callibaetis* hatch, and with good reason. A simple tie, the Gilled Nymph accurately matches the prominent gills found along the abdomen of a real *Callibaetis* nymph, and it also replicates the nymph's slim profile. Building gills into a fly without undue complications or bulk is no easy feat and Shane, in his usual magical way, found an easy method of replicating this important piece of the puzzle in a simple and stress-free way.

This pattern is hugely popular on Colorado reservoirs during the summerlong Callibaetis *hatch, but you can tie it in different colors and sizes to imitate a wide range of mayfly nymphs.*

I like to be pretty selective about the ostrich herl I use on this pattern, preferring thick, full-fibered feathers with wide herls to accentuate the gilled effect along the abdomen. Full ostrich plumes seem to be the best bet here rather than the smaller feathers often found in fly shops, so keep this in mind when shopping for your materials. Shane used the tips of the ostrich herl abdomen for the tail on his original pattern, but I have replaced them here with the somewhat finer tips of an emu feather. Emu is similar to ostrich herl, but is proportionately smaller and more streamlined on a fly like this. I have also replaced the wing case with Swiss Straw rather than the not-the-same-as-it-was Medallion Sheeting that Shane preferred. Shane, a spectacular fly tier and designer who passed away in 2011, was actually the maker of Medallion Sheeting (as well as a host of other innovative fly-tying materials), and what is currently marketed as Medallion Sheeting is thicker and stiffer than the product Shane produced. Swiss Straw makes a suitable substitute and is readily available and easy to use. The rest of the pattern is relatively straightforward and an easy tie, using common materials found at nearly any fly shop, but attention to detail and good technique must still be adhered to. Variations in color and size as well as a bead head option round out the possibilities.

I tie this pattern in sizes ranging from 12 to 18, in both tan and olive versions. *Callibaetis* can range a fair bit in color and having a few minor color variations in your fly box can be worthwhile. My favorite way to fish a *Callibaetis* nymph is with a floating line to a sighted fish, casting ahead of the trout and allowing the fly to sink to its level before beginning a slow retrieve. Many anglers simply hang these under an indicator and let them dangle, adjusting the depth until they find exactly where the fish are. I am a total failure at sitting and watching an indicator, however, and while I can sometimes calm myself down enough to do it, I much prefer a more active role—unless I'm catching fish after fish on the dangle, in which case I'll watch that indicator all day long! It can be effective to have an intermediate sink line along as well, to drag the fly a bit deeper and keep it in the zone on the retrieve. Stillwater fishing is as much about finding where the fish are in the vertical water column as where exactly they are in the lake itself. Constant up-and-down adjustment is often needed to locate the proper depth to retrieve any pattern in a situation like this, so don't be afraid to lengthen the leader, switch up fly lines, or adjust the indicator on your leader to move your flies into the path of the fish. Often it's just a matter of letting the fly sink a bit more before beginning the retrieve or sliding the indicator up or down the leader to peg the fly at a particular depth, but this is often overlooked by many anglers despite making all the difference. Adjust, adjust, adjust!

GILLED NYMPH

Hook: #12-18 TMC 200R
Thread: Tan or rusty dun 8/0 Uni
Tail: Natural emu fibers or tan ostrich herl tips
Rib: Gold UTC wire (x small)
Abdomen: Tan ostrich herl
Wing case: Brown Swiss Straw
Thorax: Tan Superfine
Legs: Natural brown Hungarian partridge fibers

1. Start the thread at the 70 percent point and wrap a smooth base back to where the thread will hang even with the barb.

2. Strip the shortest fibers from the base of an emu feather and preen the remaining fibers so they stand out from the stem a bit.

3. Select the bottom three fibers from the stem on one side and peel them off.

4. Measure the tips of the emu fibers against the hook so they are about a half shank in length. Tie the emu in at the bend of the hook and wrap forward over the butt ends to the starting point.

5. Catch the end of a length of wire under a couple thread wraps at the starting point and pull it down to length.

6. Wrap back over the wire to the base of the tail, keeping the wire along the near side of the shank as you go.

7. Select two bushy ostrich herls and clip them from the stem. Wet the tip of the feathers and preen the tip fibers forward while holding the remaining fibers back, creating a separation point.

8. Catch the separation point of the feathers with a couple wraps of thread at the bend. Wrap forward over the tip ends to anchor the feathers in place; take care to keep a smooth, level underbody as you go. Note there are no individual flues tied down at the bend of the hook and that there is a *tiny* bit (about a thread width) of space between the herl and the tail.

9. Continue wrapping forward over the tip ends of the ostrich to the starting point and clip any remaining length.

10. Grab both ostrich herls and wrap them up the hook to form a bushy abdomen. Be careful to let these wraps feed forward concentrically so they do not overlap and bind each other down. Continue wrapping the ostrich to the starting point and tie it off with a couple turns of thread.

11. Spiral-wrap the wire forward through the ostrich abdomen to the starting point and tie it off. It's hard to see the wire spacing when wrapped through this bushy abdomen so you may need to trust your instincts and wrap a bit blindly.

12. Break off the excess wire by tugging it sharply toward the bend. Clip the excess ostrich herl and wrap a thread base over the stubs and up to the eye of the hook. Return the thread to the starting point.

13. Using the tips of your sharpest scissors, come in and trim the flue fibers off the top of the body—and only the top of the body—creating a flat dorsal surface.

14. Rotate the hook in the vise a bit and do the same on the bottom. You want to leave the ostrich flues along the sides of the abdomen, but trim them off both the top and bottom to create a flattened profile. These flues will do a nice job of imitating the gills of a swimming mayfly nymph like a *Callibaetis* or Gray Drake.

15. You should now have some sparse gills along the sides of the flattened abdomen as shown here. You can use a dubbing brush to pick out any trapped fibers along the abdomen if needed. Wet you fingers and slick the ostrich herl back toward the bend for now so it doesn't get bound down during the remainder of the tying process. Wrap just slightly back over the front edge of the abdomen.

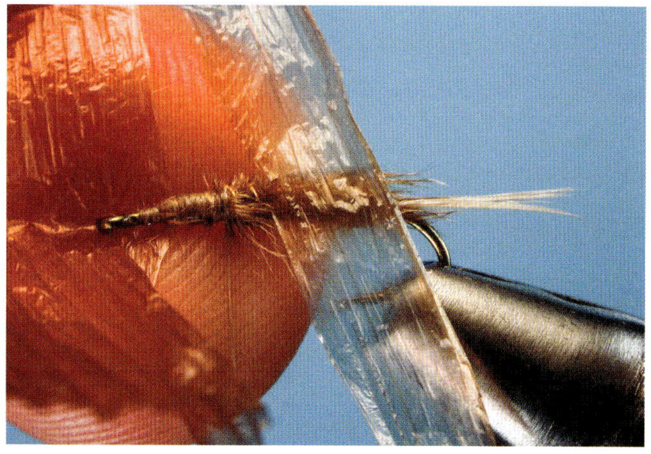

16. Cut a length of brown Swiss Straw that is about one and a half times as wide as the hook gap. We want this strip to be a little wider than normally used for a wing case because the Swiss Straw will buckle and wrinkle a bit when tied in and pulled over, creating a realistic wing case.

17. Lay the end of the Swiss Straw on the top of the hook at the front of the abdomen and hold it in place by putting the pad of your material-hand thumb on top of it and pressing down. Make sure the front end is well behind the hook eye so you don't have to trim it later.

18. Bring a loose wrap of thread up and over the Swiss Straw to catch it against the top of the hook on the front edge of the abdomen. Wrap forward over the butt ends of the wing case to anchor them down and then return to the base of the wing case and make a wrap to securely anchor it at the 60 to 65 percent point. Lift the wing case and check behind it to make sure there are no wraps of thread showing.

19. Dub a thin strand of dubbing onto the thread and start wrapping it at the back of the index point, working backward and up the taper that was left from tying in the wing case.

20. Wrap all the way back to the base of the wing case and then work forward again to the back of the index point, ending with bare thread just behind the eye. Your thorax should have a slightly descending taper to it.

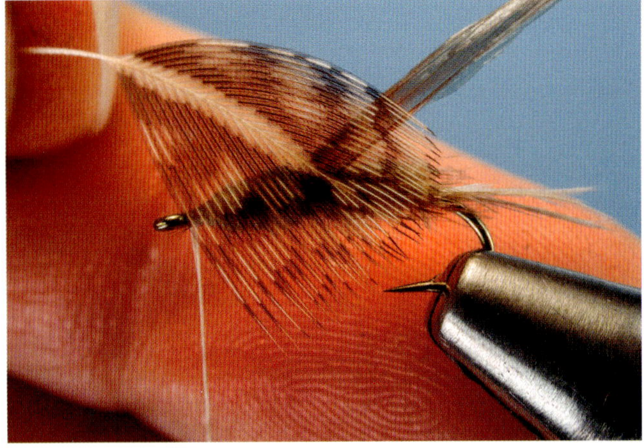

21. Select a Hungarian partridge body feather with a square end, not a rounded shape. Peel the fluff and short fibers off the stem, leaving only the fibers that form this flat end.

22. With the tips of your scissors, reach in and trim only the center stem of the partridge feather, leaving a V-shaped feather with even fibers on both sides. Lay the V end of the feather in around the hook eye with the legs of the V on either side of the shank. Slide the tips of the fibers back so they are just a touch longer than the thorax.

23. Once the tips are positioned, reach in with your material hand and pinch the legs of the V against the sides of the fly, holding them firmly in place. Note that the base of the V is beyond the hook eye here. We don't want to tie the base of the V down as that will prevent the fibers from separating into to equal bunches on either side of the fly. Make a loose wrap of thread near the crotch of the V right in front of the end of the thorax. Tighten this wrap by pulling toward you, holding the tips of the feather firmly in position all the while.

24. Make a few more tight thread turns to anchor the legs in place before releasing your grip. They should be neatly and evenly divided around the front of the thorax.

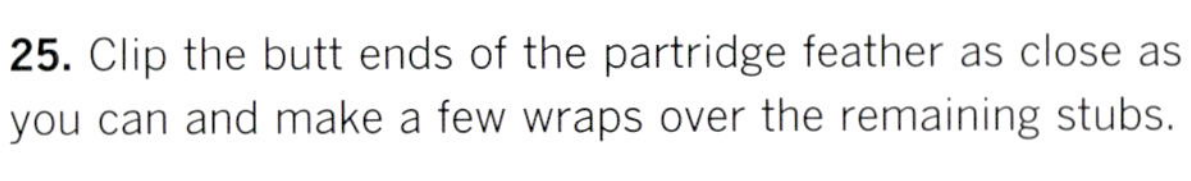

25. Clip the butt ends of the partridge feather as close as you can and make a few wraps over the remaining stubs.

26. Pull the strip of Swiss Straw forward over the thorax, letting it fold and buckle. Catch the front end of the wing case with a couple wraps of thread just behind the eye. Pinching the wide end of the Swiss Straw wing case down here with the thread wraps will create a few more creases and folds in the wing case as well as forming it tightly to the top of the thorax.

27. Fold the remaining long end of the Swiss Straw wing case back over the top and bind the fold down with a few turns of thread. Folding the wing case tie-down like this will keep it from ever pulling out from under the thread wraps.

28. Trim the remaining end of the wing case strip flush, build a smooth thread head, and whip-finish.

29. Top view. Note the flowing gills and slender body.

9

HOT WIRE PRINCE

The Hot Wire Prince has become a Colorado favorite and demonstrates the use of two colors of wire to blend into one. Take special care to create a smooth thread underbody and leave no spaces when wrapping the two-wire body.

One of the most popular patterns on many Colorado freestone rivers, the Hot Wire Prince is a proven fish catcher. I've always thought of this pattern as the obvious combination of two of the most popular trout nymphs ever: the Copper John and the Prince Nymph. Coupling a wire body with the attributes of the ubiquitous Prince Nymph creates a pattern with a few more options than either original pattern has on its own. Going a step further and using two colors of wire to create the body allows for mind-melding colors to be created. Green and yellow wire combine to create a buggy bright green color, while red and blue wrapped together make a nice purple version. There are endless color combinations thanks to all the wire colors now available at your fingertips; tying a whole boxful of Hot Wire Princes would not be considered a waste of time. I've had many good days on Colorado's Arkansas and Colorado Rivers with a Hot Wire Prince tied to my tippet. Both of these rivers are heavy with caddis larvae and pupae, and the Hot Wire does a fine job of imitating these stages.

I find this fly to be most effective when heavily weighted, and to that end I

The Hot Wire Prince can be an effective representation of anything from a small stonefly nymph to a caddis larva or pupa.

always tie mine with both a tungsten bead head and a lead wire underbody. I prefer to fish it under a dry in a dry-and-dropper rig, and I have found that heavily weighted flies get down more quickly and stay down better than their lighter-weight counterparts, as well as hang more tautly on the dropper tippet, relaying strikes much more quickly than a lighter fly on a slack line.

There's an often overlooked tidbit to keep in mind when tying this pattern (and any other with a tapered thread underbody): Be sure to smoothly taper the underbody from the bare shank up to the lead to create a nice, smooth taper to wrap the wire over. Lumpy, bumpy underbodies are always mirrored through the overbody on flies like this so it is well worth the extra time it takes to smooth out the base. If your underbody looks like crap, your overbody is going to as well.

This fly is tied just like the normal Prince Nymph pattern you're already familiar with, but with the simple addition of a wire abdomen. I always use two different-sized wires to make the body, as the small difference in wire diameter helps to create a slightly more ribbed effect on the body and leans the colors slightly more to the hue of the larger wire. Think of the smaller strand of wire as a highlight and the larger strand as the primary fly color.

While the conventional Prince Nymph was indeed originally tied with the turned-up biot horns seen here, this little variation has fallen out of favor with most tiers over the years. For exactly that reason, I make sure to tie all of my Hot Wire Princes with the horns curving up and away from the body just so I feel like I am fishing something a little different than the last guy through the riffle. No, it probably doesn't make any difference to the fish, but it does in my head and we all know that means a lot.

When you break this fly down, it really does have a lot going for it. Its realistic biot tail can cross over to imitate a small stonefly nymph while still being reasonably similar to the claspers on the back end of a caddis nymph. It has a durable and colorful wire body coupled with fish catching peacock herl and a lively soft hackle collar. The white horns on the front of this fly and on the original Prince Nymph have always stymied me as to exactly what they imitate, but apparently the fish love them and they do add an air of sophistication to what would otherwise be a pretty plain pattern, so I like that part too.

The Hot Wire can be an effective representation of anything from a small stonefly nymph to a caddis larva or pupa. Endless color combinations make it a natural to help fill your fly box and the wire body makes it a bit more interesting to tie than a standard Prince Nymph. I carry them in the yellow-and-green combo as well as in brown and gold and pink and silver. This range covers both caddis and stones well and the pink version serves as a good attractor nymph. Olive and brown, red and yellow, blue and red, and chartreuse and silver are other popular color combinations.

HOT WIRE PRINCE

Hook: #10-18 TMC 3761
Bead: Gold-colored tungsten or brass, sized to hook
Weight: Lead or nonlead wire, sized to hook
Thread: Black 8/0 Uni
Tail: Brown goose biots
Abdomen: Green (Brassie) and hot yellow (small) UTC Wire
Thorax: Peacock herl
Hackle: Brown hen neck hackle
Horns: White goose biots

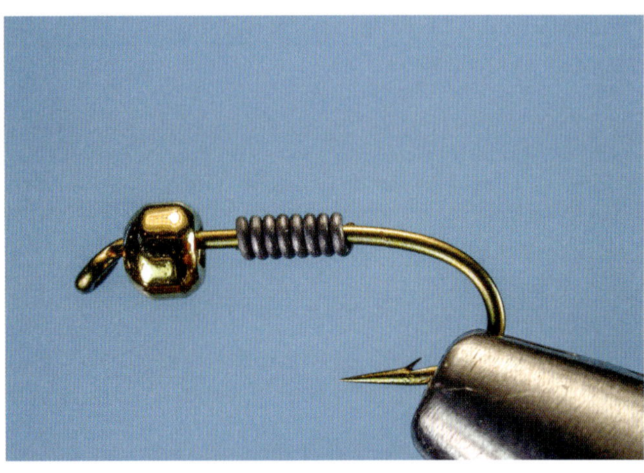

1. Place the bead on the hook and slide it up to the eye. Mount the hook in the vise and make eight or ten wraps of lead wire around the hook shank. Break the ends of the wire off flush against the shank.

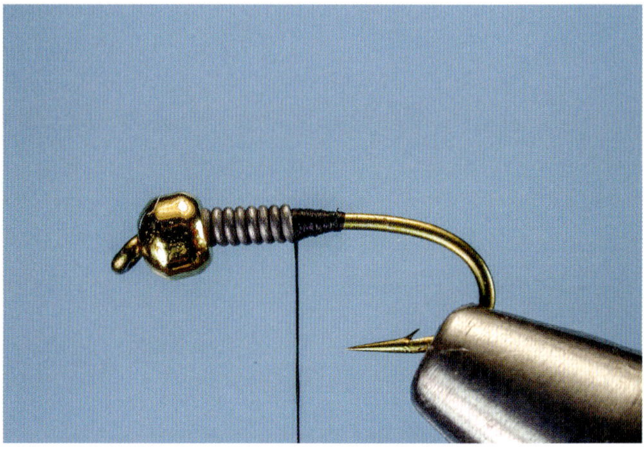

2. Shove the lead wraps up into the back of the bead, countersinking the first couple turns into the recess in the back of the bead. These wraps add weight to the fly and help to center the bead on the hook shank. Start the thread behind the lead wraps and build a small thread dam from the bare shank up to the diameter of the lead.

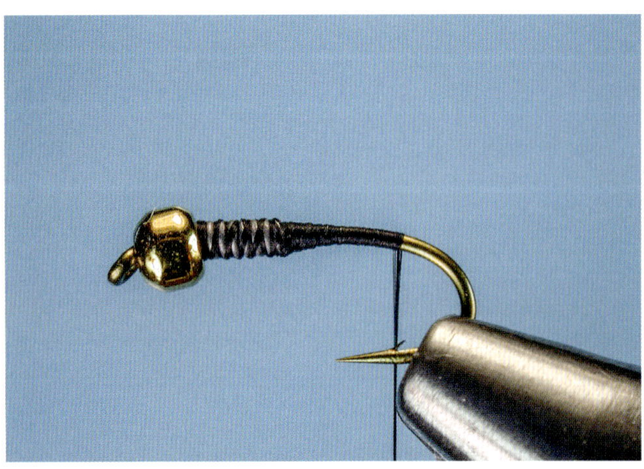

3. Wrap the thread forward over the lead to the back of the bead and then back down the shank again to the bend of the hook, creating a thread base as you go. Leave the thread hanging even with the point on the barb.

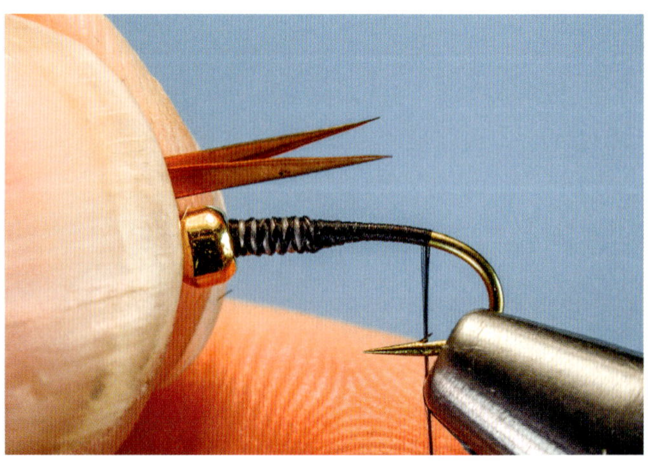

4. Select two brown goose biots and oppose their curves. Measure the matched biots against the shank so they are just a touch longer than half a shank.

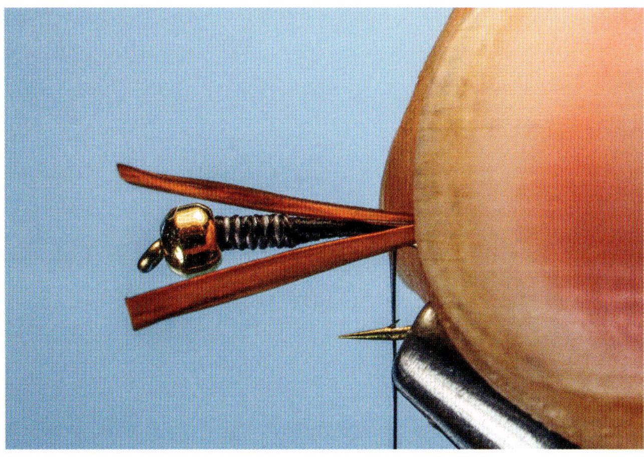

5. Grasp the measured tips of the biots in your material hand and place them on either side of the hook shank. Simply pinch them in place, but rather than holding them directly atop the shank where we want them to end up, we want to hold them rotated just slightly toward the near side of the shank.

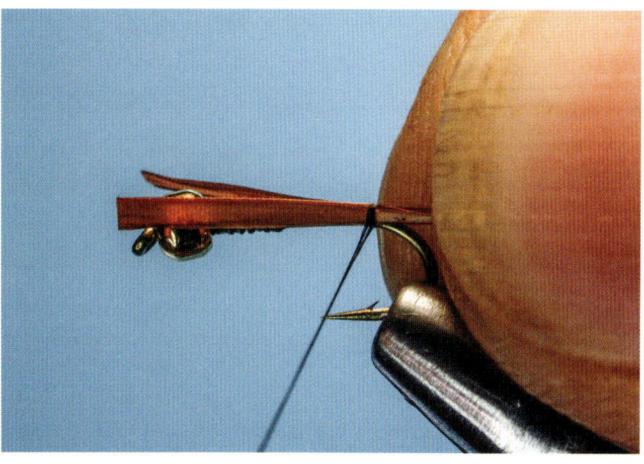

6. Take a single turn of thread over both biots at the bend of the hook. This wrap is taut but not yet tightened and should only begin to compress the biots against the hook. Make one more taut turn of thread over the first wrap.

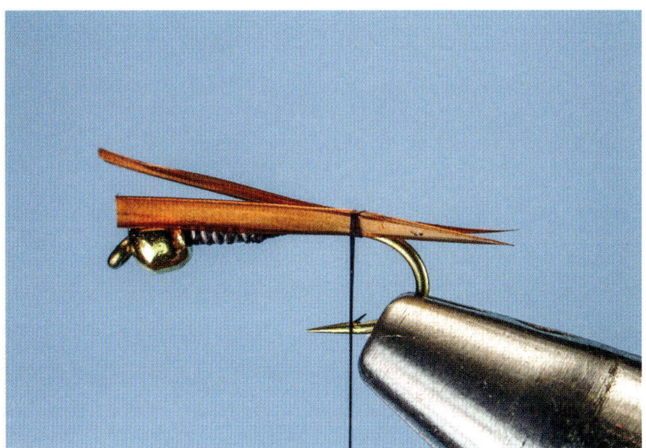

7. I generally advise folks not to let go of the tips of the biots right here, but I had to get my hand out of the way so you could see what's going on. The biots ought to be lashed to the hook, not tightly, nor in the correct position, but rather just held in place with two wraps of thread and slightly tilted to the near side of the hook.

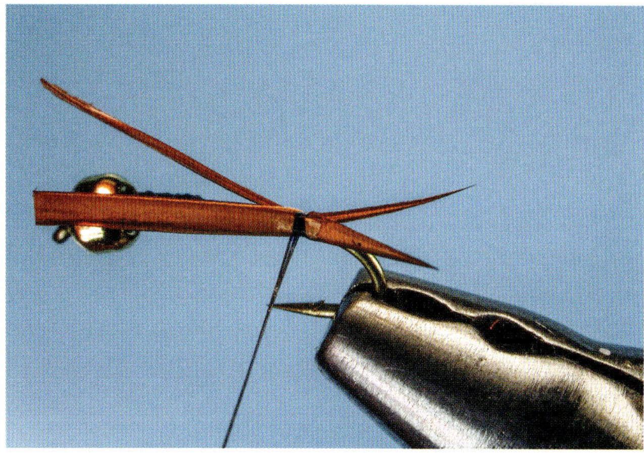

8. Draw the thread toward you to tighten the thread wraps and watch as the biots start to roll into position on the top dead center of the hook. Stop pulling on the thread when the biots are properly positioned.

9. Wrap forward over the biots just up onto the back of the lead wraps, anchoring them firmly in place as you go. Be sure that no thread turns go behind the first two wraps you put over the biots so as not to disrupt their placement.

10. Clip the excess butt ends of the biots flush against the hook shank. Leave the thread hanging at the tie-off point. Cut a length of wire from each color and even their tips. Lay these two pieces next to the shank at a slight angle as shown here.

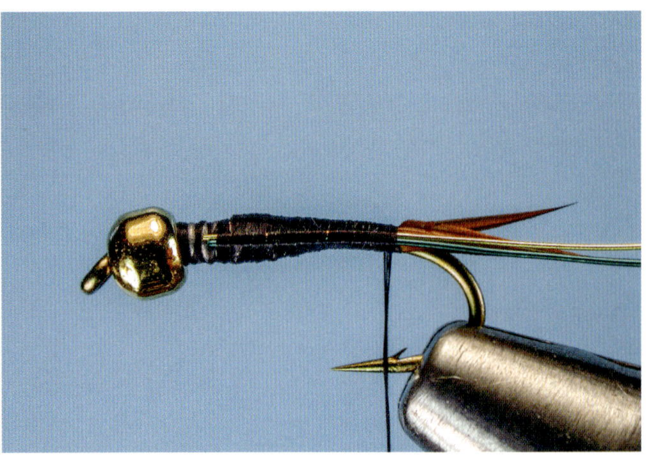

11. Capture the ends of the wire with a couple turns of thread, and then align both strands so they lay along the near side of the hook. Begin to wrap tightly back over the wire toward the bend of the hook. Continue wrapping over the wire with the thread all the way to the base of the tails. Be sure to make the thread wraps extra tight as you near the bend; this keeps the wire from trying to crawl up and over the shank when you start to wrap it.

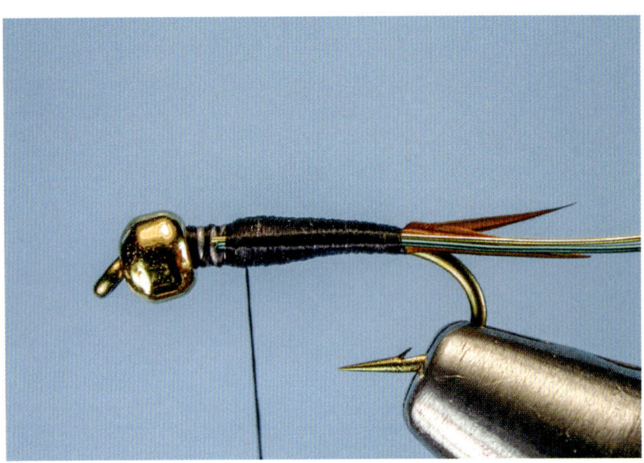

12. Work the thread forward again from the bend, building a smooth, tapered underbody as you go. Don't make this underbody too fat—keep in mind that the wire is still going to be wrapped over the top and will thicken the body more. Leave the thread hanging where you tied in the wire.

13. Lift both pieces of wire as one unit and bring them over the hook shank. Bring both pieces of wire down on the far side of the hook and up again from the bottom to complete the first turn of wire. You may need to shove these wraps rearward with your fingernail if they don't butt right up to the base of the tail. Continue wrapping both strands forward, taking care to keep the wraps butted against the previous turn so that you are leaving no spaces.

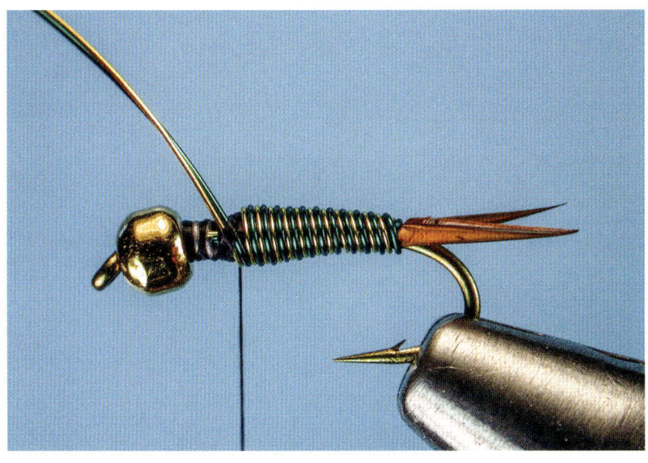

14. Wrap the wires all the way up to the starting point and tie them off with a few tight thread wraps. If your underbody was nice and smooth and you paid close attention and the moon was in the right phase and you held your mouth just right, you ought to have a nicely tapered and smooth two-toned abdomen about now.

15. Helicopter the ends of the wire to break them off flush. Make a turn of thread onto the front edge of the abdomen and leave the thread hanging there.

16. Select three or four nice, bushy peacock herls, clip their tips even, and lay them against the hook where the thread is hanging. Capture the tips of the herls with a couple wraps of thread, then move the thread forward to the back of the bead.

17. Wrap the peacock herls forward three or four turns and tie them off at the back of the bead. Clip the excess butt ends flush.

18. Select, size, and prep a brown hen neck feather. You want a feather with fibers that will reach to somewhere between the point on the hook and the point on the barb. Clip the fluff from the end of the feather where the stem evens out and becomes consistent in diameter. Clip the fibers off each side of the base of the feather, leaving little barbs that will help anchor the feather in place.

19. Lay the feather along the near side or top of the shank—with the inside of the feather toward the hook shank—and anchor it down with several tight turns of thread. I like to twist my thread a bit before tying the feather down so the thread will bite in and grab the feather more tightly. As you can see here, I have left a tiny bit of the butt end sticking out in front of the thread wraps to further anchor the butt end.

20. Grab the tip of the feather in your hackle pliers and lift it straight and tight above the hook. Wet the tips of your fingers; using the "O" technique highlighted in the Soft-Hackle steps, fold the hackle fibers back along the stem toward the bend of the hook.

21. Preen the fibers back along the shank toward the bend as you pull forward on the stem in the hackle pliers. You are trying to crease the feather fibers into a "V" along their stem. Repeat the folding process until the fibers lie back to the rear of the stem.

22. Begin wrapping the hen feather around the shank between the front edge of the peacock thorax and the back edge of the bead. There is not much room here, nor should there be, so try to keep the wraps upright as you go.

23. Make about three turns of hackle, sweeping each turn back slightly before making the next one.

24. Tie off the tip of the feather with a couple tight wraps at the immediate back edge of the bead. Clip the tip of the feather off flush.

25. Reach in from the front of the hook and pinch the hackle tightly down around the bead and shank. Pinching like this will roll the stem back slightly and help to crease the fibers into place, splaying them nicely and sweeping them back along the shank. Hold these fibers in place before moving to the next step.

26. Bring your material hand from the back of the hook and grab the pinched hackle fibers and hold them down; keep them evenly distributed around the shank as you do this. Make a couple wraps of thread over the base of the wrapped hackle to hold these fibers back.

27. Once you let go the fly should look a lot like this.

28. Select two white goose biots from near the base of the feather (where they are a bit wider). Do not oppose these two biots, but rather, cross them like scissor blades with their intersection point lined up immediately behind the bead and their tips extending to the base of the tail. I like to tie my regular Princes with the biots curving down, but for some unknown reason I always tie my Hot Wire Princes with the biots curving up. Again, it's your call, but I'm just saying all the cool kids tie them curving up. Lay the biots on top of the thread band between the bead and the hackle and check their length against the hook. Press your thumb down on top of the biots, pushing them against the top of the hook shank.

29. Roll your thumb back slightly toward the eye of the hook; then press the tip of your material-hand thumb onto the tips of the biots to hold them in place and to length.

30. With your thumb still pressed tightly against the biots, spin your bobbin to tighten the thread into a cord. Then make a couple wraps over the biots at the *rear edge* of the thread band between the hackle and the bead.

31. Here is a close-up of the wrap placement. We have about three thread widths of space to work with and we want these wraps on the biots to be at the back edge of this space.

32. Use your finest-tipped scissors to trim the butt ends of the biots flush against the back of the bead. By tying the biots in at the rear edge of this space, we have allowed for the inherent stub ends left by the scissors and left room to cover them with a few well-placed wraps of thread *behind* the bead.

33. Make those few, well-placed wraps of thread to cover those stub ends smoothly—it only takes a couple turns. Keep in mind you still have to whip-finish; the wraps of the actual whip can be used to further cover any remaining stubs. In other words, don't make fifty turns of thread here; just get them covered with well-placed wraps and whip-finish. Clip the thread.

34. The white biots ought to be about 45 degrees apart and the body should be smooth and seamless if you want to catch the big fish. I find anything less than 42 degrees to be the preferred food of dinks and tiddlers.

10

PIGSTICKER

What the Pigsticker lacks in beauty it makes up for with its incredible effectiveness. While it seems simple to tie, a few details like keeping your thread flattened and smooth and proper placement of the lead wraps are important considerations.

Everyone I know likes to make fun of this fly. It's not exactly pretty, nor is it complicated. Even if it were both of those things, the fact remains that it imitates a lowly worm. Yet the Pigsticker really is one of my favorite flies. While a traditional San Juan Worm pattern tied with chenille will fill the requisite (and sometimes hidden) worm compartment in your fly box, I find the Pigsticker to be more useful for a variety of reasons. The fact that I can easily weight a Pigsticker, from slightly weighted to quite heavily, makes this pattern my go-to annelid imitation. While a conventional San Juan Worm can be fished as a dropper, its inherent lack of weight often keeps it tethered behind a heavier fly. The Pigsticker, on the other hand, makes a fantastic dropper under a dry, can be used as the weighted pattern in a hopper-copper-dropper rig, or can even be fished alone without additional weight in a conventional nymphing rig under an indicator.

The unusual hook supplies a good portion of the magic of this pattern. Originally tied on a Mustad 37160 "Kahle" hook, the modern equivalent is the sticky-sharp Gamakatsu C12U. The arched hump of both of these hooks,

Even though some make fun of the Pigsticker, I have to admit that an awful lot of the biggest fish I have ever caught in rivers have fallen to this fly.

There are a few little tricks to tying this fly and a couple things to watch out for. Be sure to keep the fly as smoothly tapered as you can, and cover all the lead wraps with thread as you tie. I prefer to use 140-denier or even 210-denier UTC thread for tying this pattern, as these larger threads build much more efficiently and smoothly than the more standard 70 denier. Of course you can tie the thing with 70 denier, but I am telling you now, you'll be there all day. Get some bigger thread in a few colors and do it right.

as well as that of the now unavailable TMC 205BL, creates a squirming worm shape and is an excellent hooking tool. The Gamakatsu comes only as big as a size 6, while the Mustad is still available in much bigger sizes up to 2 and beyond. The Gammy size 6 is about perfect for most of my uses and truthfully, it's really about the only size I worry about. I do tie some of the flies more heavily weighted than the others for use in faster or deeper water, and I tie them in a range of colors, too: red with a silver wire rib, orange with silver wire, brown with copper wire, rusty orange with copper . . . the variations are endless and all of them work.

While most folks look at this fly and think it imitates a garden worm, there really is an aquatic version that lives in the river bottom and gets washed out during higher flows. An aquatic annelid looks just like the regular garden-variety worm save for being flat along one side. Luckily, this small difference doesn't require any special tying procedures and a simple round-bodied fly still works wonders. All the fish I catch on this fly mistake it for the natural's aquatic version rather than something you'd dig up in your backyard.

Although this fly will catch fish even with the lead wraps showing through—as proven often and loudly by my good friend Luke Bever—none of these fish count in your daily total and are actually deducted from your tally under the heading of "carelessness." Be sure to keep the fly tapering down to a quite thin width at either end; again, this better replicates a real worm and keeps the fly from looking like a length of red licorice in your box. This fly is simple and quick as it is but that's no reason to leave it looking bad out of laziness (even if you really are lazy). Be sure to cover the thread body and rib with some sort of coating. Sally Hansen's Hard As Nails has been a perennial favorite, and Clear Cure Goo Hydro is coming on strong as well. The flattened-thread body will fray easily if not coated and as such, it's important to toughen the body up a bit with one of these coatings. In a pinch, even several coats of head cement will work okay—just be sure to let each dry before adding the next.

PIGSTICKER

Hook: #6-10 Gamakatsu C12U
Weight: .015- or .020-inch diameter lead or nonlead wire
Thread: Red 140- or 210-denier UTC Ultra Thread
Rib: Silver UTC Ultra Wire (small)
Coating: Clear Cure Goo Hydro, Sally Hansen's Hard As Nails, Hard As Hull, or Gloss Coat

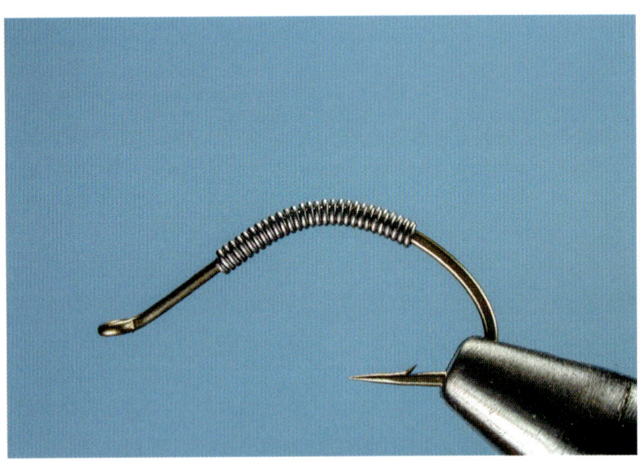

1. Begin by making from ten to thirty turns of lead wire on the hook shank. Start at the back of the hook and wrap the wire forward. I prefer to use a few more wraps of the .015 lead rather than fewer of the .020 to help keep the fly a bit on the skinny side. Regardless of how many turns of wire you make, center them along the hump on the shank in order to leave some bare hook exposed at either end of the lead wraps.

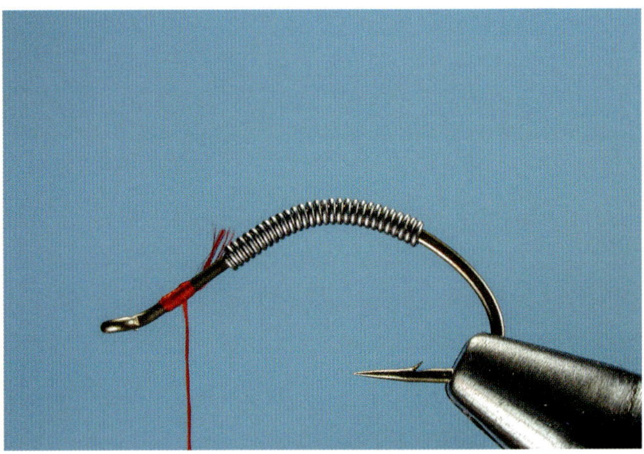

2. Start the tying thread about two eye lengths back from the eye. It is important to keep the thread lying as flat as possible on a Pigsticker; this helps cover the lead wraps and produces a smoothly tapered body.

3. Wrap up to the front end of the lead wraps, building a small thread dam as you go. The thread should taper up smoothly to the diameter of the lead wraps.

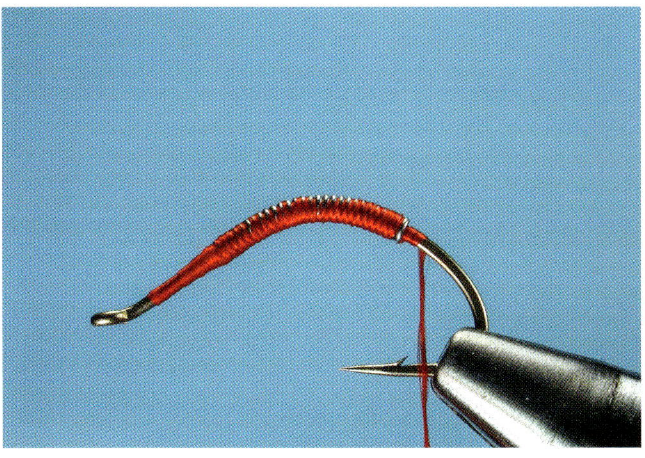

4. Spin your bobbin to flatten the thread out some more and continue wrapping back over the lead wraps. You don't need to entirely cover the lead wraps on this pass, as we will be making another trip forward to finish off the shape, but keep that thread lying as flat and smooth as you can and cover the lead as much as you can without building too much bulk. Bring the thread down onto the bare shank at the back of the lead wraps for a couple flat turns.

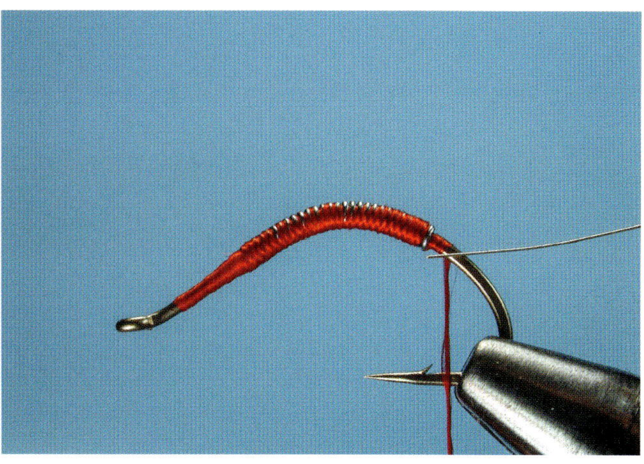

5. Place the end of a piece of ribbing wire up against the back of the lead.

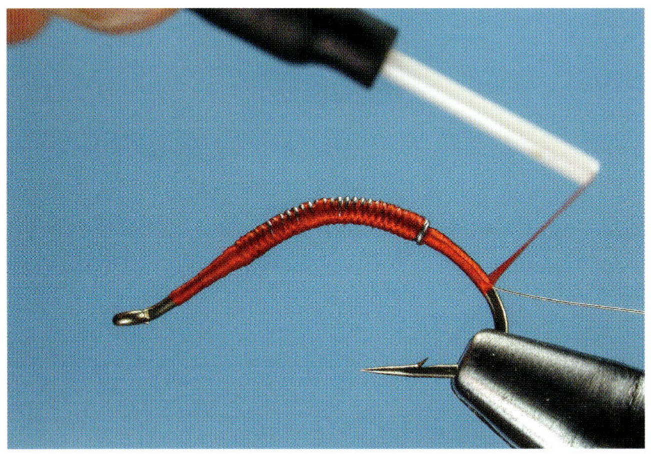

6. Catch the end of the ribbing wire under a few wraps of thread and continue wrapping back down toward the bend of the hook. Keep the wire in line with the hook shank along the near side as you wrap over it. Wrap back on the hook until the thread is even with the hook eye if you were to draw a line through the hook gap from the bottom of the hook eye to the bend.

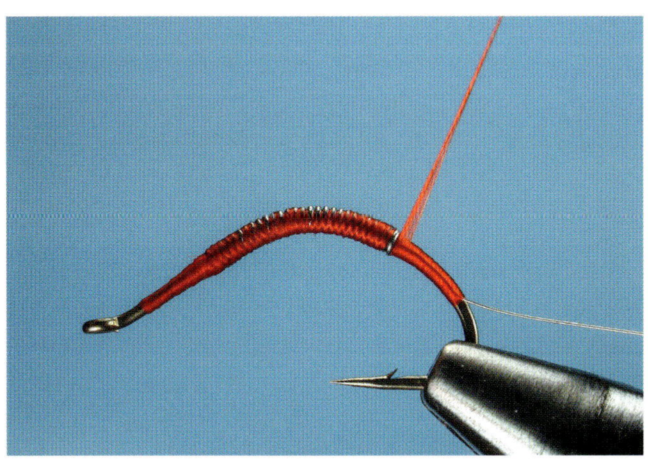

7. Flatten the thread once more by spinning the bobbin, and then wrap forward again to the back of the lead wraps. Build a taper up to the lead diameter as you work forward.

8. Wrap up to and on to the lead wraps and continue forward, this time completely covering the lead wraps with a smoothly tapered layer of thread.

9. Wrap forward over the lead all the way to the front of the hook, taking care to maintain that smooth shape right up to the eye of the hook.

10. Spiral-wrap the ribbing wire forward over the thread body with about ten turns. Tie the wire off at the back of the hook eye with a couple firm thread wraps. Helicopter the end of the wire to break it off flush.

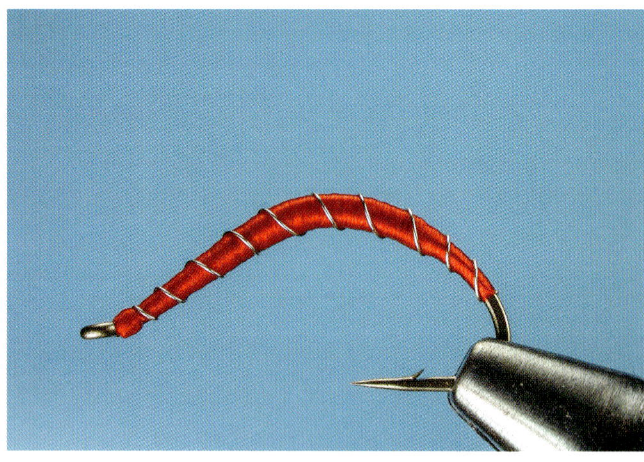

11. Build a smooth thread head over the wire stub and whip-finish the thread.

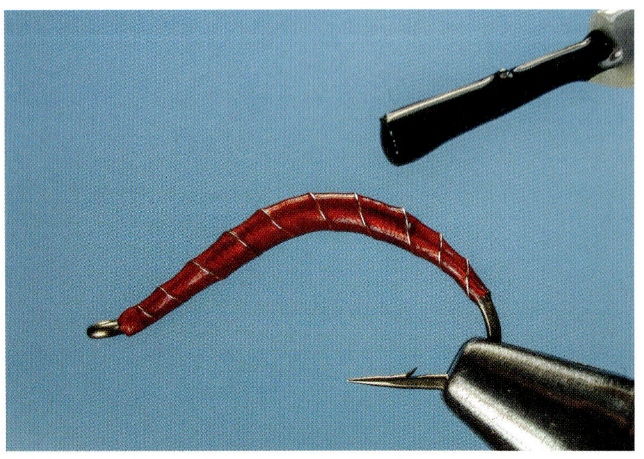

12. Coat all sides of the fly with your favorite coating. I often use plain Gloss Coat head cement or Sally Hansen's Hard As Nails; I make a single heavy coat to start and then set the fly aside to dry in a block of foam before adding a second coat. If you use CCG Hydro, one coat is all that is necessary and you actually have to be a little careful about building it up too much.

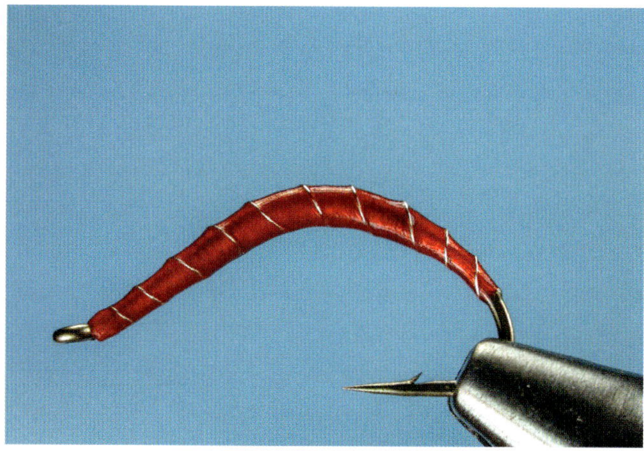

13. Finished fly. No lumps or bumps or corded up thread and no lead showing through is what you should be shooting for here.

ANNELID

Hook: Gamakatsu C12U #10-16
Thread: Red 70-denier UTC
Underbody: Red Flashabou
Overbody: Red Micro Tubing

SAN JUAN WORM

Hook: #12-16 TMC 3769
Thread: Red 140-denier UTC
Worm: Red Ultra Chenille
Note: Burn the ends so it looks like you put a little effort into it.

ROCKWORM

Hook: #12-16 Daiichi 1760
Thread: Red 70-denier UTC
Body: Red D-Rib (small)

11

QUASIMODO PHEASANT TAIL

Think of the Quasi as a regular Pheasant Tail on steroids: It may not be quite as pretty, but when the real work starts it's good to have around. This fly has a lot going on, and it is important to pay close attention to proportions as you tie it.

Let's face it: There are an awful lot of fancy fly patterns out there these days and a lot of them fill the same niche. Subtle differences in materials and design create patterns that are often similar to existing ones, yet with a different enough look to turn the eye of a fish that has seen everything—and in the same vein, different enough to keep the tier and the angler interested as well. Half the fun of tying and fishing is figuring out which patterns work best for you and your type of fishing. I just happen to be one of those guys who loves flies in general, so it's pretty hard for me to opt out of anything, and the time-proven and well-worn Pheasant Tail still has a spot in my box.

I featured the conventionally tied American Pheasant Tail in my first book, so I thought I'd change things up a bit here and show what has become one of the pattern's most popular variations: the Quasimodo Pheasant Tail. Differing

While I use the conventional Pheasant Tail as a more accurate mayfly nymph representation for pickier fish, I find that I opt for the Quasi more as a searching pattern—its overall shape is a bit meatier and the addition of both the bead and the flash lend it better to probing and searching than the sparsely dressed original.

from the original in hook selection and weighting and the addition of a bead and a flashback, the "Quasi" brings a new, slightly chunkier profile to an already effective fly pattern. There are, of course, several differences in the techniques required to tie the fly in this manner, and that is reason enough to add it to your repertoire. These added design elements work together to create a fly that fishes well in entirely different applications than the original.

While the typical transformation from standard-issue to bead head is usually simple, in this case the fly really takes on a whole new look and use. It's still a Pheasant Tail by recipe, but dressed up with a few modifications to make it more useable across a wider range of fishing conditions. In my box, the bead is always tungsten (when I use the word "bead" in these recipes, I am referring to a tungsten bead). I frankly see no reason to tie anything with a plain brass bead anymore, as the tungsten beads are so much heavier. If there is one thing I have learned over the years, it's that it is really hard to make a small fly too heavy.

In addition to the tungsten bead, I add a few wraps of lead wire. This lead serves two purposes: It adds weight and helps center the bead on the hook shank. Just a few turns of lead, tucked into the recess in the back of the bead, will align the bead correctly on the hook behind the eye so it doesn't sag or require a hundred wraps of thread to fill in. I use this little trick on nearly all my bead head flies these days. The Quasimodo Pheasant Tail also features a relatively unique flashback wing case and a back strip. While flash is not always necessary and can even be a liability at times, for the purposes of where and when I fish this fly, I really prefer the flashy version.

While the standard Pheasant Tail is a near-perfect match for a slim mayfly nymph like a *Baetis* or PMD, the Quasi's thickened outline definitely leans more toward a small stonefly nymph. The weight and flash make the Quasi a bit more versatile from a fishing standpoint. The weight of the bead keeps the fly drifting a bit deeper and makes it a more viable candidate to hang under a dry, and that little extra bit of flash down the back can be effective at catching a cynical fish's eye.

While the American Pheasant Tail is properly tied using only four strands of pheasant tail fibers, the Quasimodo's thickened profile requires a fair bit more material. I do indeed tie these on the chunkier side, and to that end use a generous bunch of fibers for the tail and abdomen. The larger sizes I typically tie this fly in require more material to cover the shank and build each section of the fly. I have become fond of mixing things up a bit by tying these with dyed pheasant tail fibers as well. Black, olive, red, yellow, and orange dyed pheasant tail all make great attractor patterns and add a bit of color to your options.

QUASIMODO PHEASANT TAIL

Hook: #8-18 TMC 2457 or 2488H
Bead: Copper tungsten, sized to hook
Thread: Camel 8/0 Uni
Weight (optional): Lead or nonlead wire, sized to hook
Tail: Natural ring-necked pheasant tail barbs
Rib: Copper wire, sized to hook
Abdomen: Natural ring-necked pheasant tail barbs
Flashback: Pearl Hedron Fire Fly
Wing case: Natural ring-necked pheasant tail barbs
Thorax: Peacock herl
Legs: Natural ring-necked pheasant tail tips

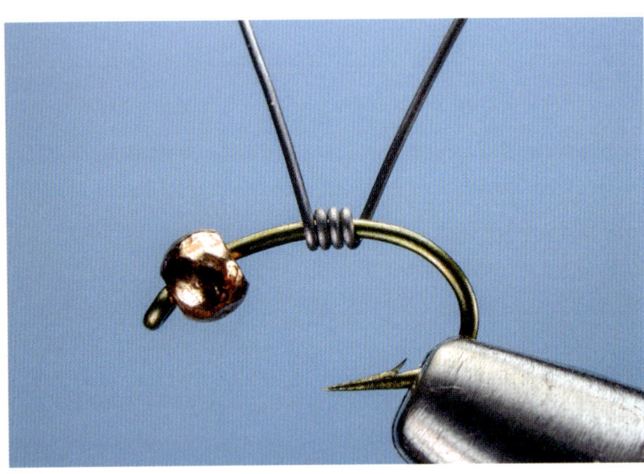

1. Slide the bead onto the hook and up to the eye. Mount the hook in the vise and make about four turns of lead wire around the shank right in the middle. These wraps will add a bit of weight, but even more importantly, they will help to center the bead on the shank and fatten up the thorax a bit.

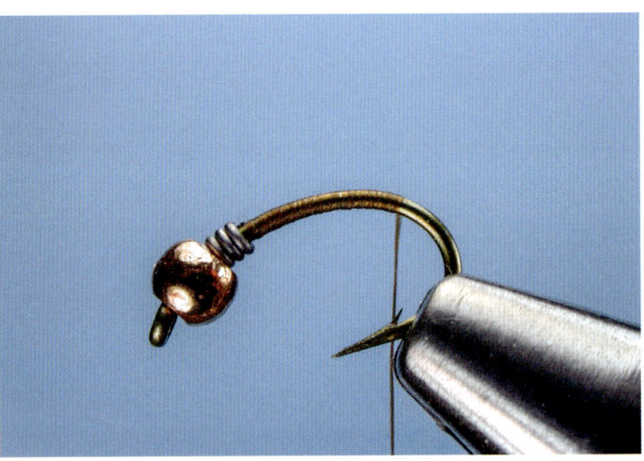

2. Break the ends off the lead wraps with your fingernail and make sure the ends are tucked in tight against the hook shank. Use your fingernail or the tips of the outside of your scissor blades to smooth the ends down if needed. We don't want any stub ends sticking out of the body. Shove the lead wraps up into the back of the bead. Brass beads have a deeper countersink than tungsten beads, and as such, the lead wraps will go deeper into a brass bead than they will into a tungsten bead. Start the tying thread at the back of the lead wraps and wrap a smooth thread base down around the curve of the hook, as shown here.

3. Select six or eight natural ring-necked pheasant tail fibers and preen them out from the stem so their tips are even; then strip them from the stem. Measure the tips against the shank of the hook so they are about a half shank long.

4. Tie the pheasant tail fibers in at the bend of the hook to create a tail that is about a half shank long. Wrap forward over the butt ends of the pheasant fibers up to the back of the lead wraps. We want to wrap over them all the way up the shank to keep a consistent diameter to the hook shank; this will create a more shapely body with no lumps or bumps. Clip the excess pheasant fibers off flush at the back of the lead wraps.

5. Tilt the vise slightly toward you, or just simply sit up straight so you can see the top of the hook shank well. Tie in a single strand of pearl Fire Fly flash at the back of the lead wraps right on top of the shank.

6. Hold the flash ever so slightly toward your near side as you wrap back over it with the thread to the base of the tail. Leave the thread hanging here for the moment and try to do this step with just one smooth layer of thread from front to back.

7. Lay a piece of copper wire at an angle to the shank at the bend as shown here. The wire should end just short of the lead wraps. Again, we're going to tie this in along the length of the abdomen (and then some) to ensure we have a smooth, even underbody that won't make our fly look like a lumpy mess.

8. Catch the end of the wire with the thread at the bend and wrap smoothly forward over it to the base of the lead. Try to keep the wire along the near side of the shank as you do this, and definitely don't let it creep up to the top of the shank as you wrap.

9. Wrap the thread again, *smoothly* back to the base of the tail. Select another half-dozen pheasant tail fibers and try to even their tips like you did for the tail. It's not a huge deal if they are not perfectly even, as the tips will get buried in our underbody, but in this case it's just going to make catching them under the thread easier. Tie this clump in at the base of the tail, but not right at their tips—they are fine and will break off easily, and this will cause bouts of swearing and throwing things, which is never good. Move the fibers up and slightly away from the tips, and anchor them in place with a couple tight wraps right at the bend.

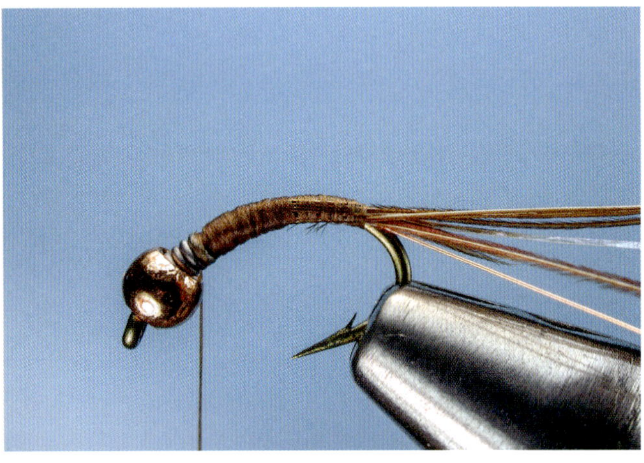

10. Now continue wrapping forward over the tips, building a slight taper with the thread (on the larger-sized flies in particular) up the back of the lead wraps. You should have a robust underbody taper here, but don't get carried away. Tiers have a tendency to tie things fatter than they want most of the time, so remember to keep it under control during this step.

11. Begin wrapping the pheasant tail fibers forward up the shank. Try to keep them lying flat like a ribbon, six or eight across, to create a nice, even abdomen.

12. Continue wrapping the pheasant fibers forward just up onto the back of the lead wraps over the tapered thread underbody. You can now finally see that the smooth, skinny underbody is paying off with a shapely, supermodel-esque tapered body. Tie the pheasant tail fibers off on top of the last couple lead wraps and clip the excess.

13. Pull the Fire Fly flash forward over the abdomen and tie it off at the front with a couple tight turns of thread. Do not clip the excess flash yet.

14. Reverse-wrap the wire rib forward over the abdomen and the flash, taking pains to keep the flash centered on the top of the shank as you spiral-wrap the wire forward.

15. Tie the wire off with a couple tight turns at the front of the abdomen. Helicopter the end to break it off and clip the excess flash. The reason we waited to clip the flash is that the wire ribbing can and does tighten that strip of flash over the top of the abdomen. Had we trimmed it flush, there would be the possibility of pulling the front end out from under the thread wraps when we wrap the ribbing.

16. Cut three strands of Fire Fly flash (about three inches long) and lay them on top of the hook with the center of their length even with the hanging thread. I prefer the Fire Fly flash for this type of pattern, as this product is slightly crimped and a bit softer than the usual Flashabou. Its inherent suppleness makes it shape to the wing case better, holding its humped shape rather than creating a flat, straight line of flash over the wing case.

17. Capture the center of the flash with a few tight turns of thread on the front edge of the abdomen.

18. Pull the front ends of the flash back over the body and wrap back over all six strands to the point on the hook. Try to keep these strands splayed out horizontally as you wrap back over them to create a wider flashback on the finished fly. You don't want six strands stacked on top of each other; instead, they should be spread out a bit across the dorsal surface of the wing case to come.

19. Select six pheasant tail fibers for the wing case, tie them in by their tips, and wrap back over them to the hook point. Keep a smooth base here, as it is the foundation for the upcoming thorax. Note that there is a tiny bit of space at the rear edge of bead. We'll need that space later, so make sure it's there.

20. Select about a half-dozen peacock herls from just below the eye of the feather. You can use the larger strung peacock herl on larger flies, but I prefer the more appropriately sized herl from the eye for smaller flies. Clip the herl tips square and a bit back from their ends and tie them in just behind the bead. Avoid tying them in by their fine tips, which break easily. Wrap back over the herls to the base of the wing case, and then forward again to just behind the bead.

Make about three turns with the peacock herl, up to the back edge of the bead, and tie them off. Don't get carried away with the herl—remember, an appropriately sized herl and thorax should be just a bit fatter than the abdomen. Clip the excess herl and take a couple thread turns over the stubs in that nearly bare spot right behind the bead.

21. For the legs, even the tips of six or eight pheasant tail fibers and strip them from the stem. Divide them three to a side in your fingertips as shown here. (They are maybe less "divided" than they are merely separated within your fingertips.) Lay the tips in from the front of the hook so their tips reach back just slightly past the end of the thorax with three fibers on each side. Note that I have not placed the fibers square on the sides of the fly, but rather the near side is a bit low and the far side a bit high to accommodate the thread torque that will pull the near-side legs up and the far-side legs down. Think ahead and adjust as needed; that's the whole secret to this fly-tying thing. Also notice that my middle finger is braced against the vise as I position the legs. Always try to brace your hand when placing materials, as it's hard to hold things in place with free-floating fingers.

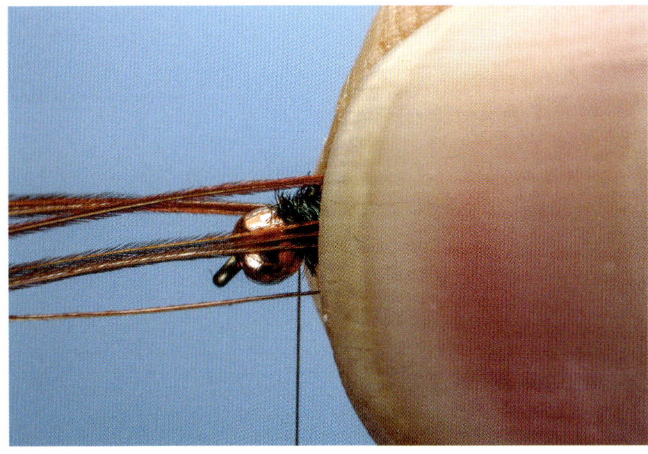

22. Now reach in with the fingertips of your material hand and grasp the measured tips in place behind the bead. Make sure they are still slightly canted toward the near side.

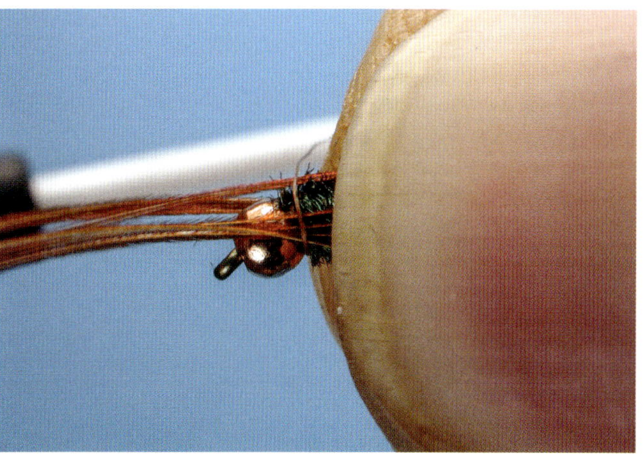

23. Bring a loose wrap of thread up and over the hook and around the legs without disturbing their angled placement.

24. Draw this wrap of thread tight by pulling it toward you underneath and on the near side of the hook. The rotation of the thread torque will pull the legs into place along the sides of the thorax. Follow up with two more tight wraps to lock them down in place directly across from each other on either side of the hook.

25. Use the tips of your finest scissors to trim the butt ends of the legs off as close to the back of the bead as you can.

26. Lift the pheasant tail fiber wing case up and separate it from the flash. Pull the wing case forward over the top of the thorax, taking pains to keep the fibers lying flat across the top of the peacock herl with no twists. You want a flat sheet across the top of the thorax, not a strip. Bind the wing case fibers down behind the bead with a couple tight wraps—now you see why we left that tiny bit of space behind the bead. Note that the fibers are spread across the top of the peacock herl and are not bunched or twisted.

27. Lift all six strands of flash; as before, try to keep them lying flat over the top of the pheasant tail wing case as you draw them forward toward the bead. Of course, with six strands, there will be some overlap, but try to keep the strands *flat* and not twisted. Catch the flash under a couple wraps of thread behind the bead as well. You can pull on the long ends a bit to maneuver the flashback and spread it out slightly if need be. Clip the flash and the stub ends of the pheasant tail wing case flush, wrap a smooth thread head over the butts, and whip-finish.

28. Keep the thread "head" behind the bead smooth and well placed. Don't build up too many turns of thread here; this band of thread should be smaller in diameter than the back of the bead. This will help keep it tight and in place when fished, and because it will actually hold together better, it will also keep you from having to tie a hundred of these for your box. My gift to you.

29. Top view of the finished fly. Take note of the thorax and abdomen proportions here and check to make sure both the backstrap flash and wingcase are taut and centered across the top of the fly.

The Quasi is a perfect fly to have on when covering lots of water in a drift boat. I will often fish it with a more imitative pattern on an indicator rig, or hang it off the back of a buoyant dry fly.

12

PAT'S RUBBER LEGS

One of the most popular "new" patterns of the last ten years, the Pat's Rubber Legs is a super effective stonefly nymph pattern that doesn't take all day to tie. Proper spacing of the legs and a dense chenille body are paramount to getting it right.

I hate this silly fly. There are so many great stonefly nymph patterns out there in the world today with beautifully mottled wing cases, accurate tails and legs, and graceful abdomens. Half the fun of tying up a big stone imitation is the pile of great materials it takes to tie one and the imaginative process that goes on in your head during the tying process. Pat's Rubber Legs is simply an affront to my artistic side and if the dang thing didn't catch fish like a heron in a fish hatchery, I wouldn't have included it in this book.

All kidding aside, the Pat's Rubber Legs, while sporting a new name these days, has been around a long time in one form or another. Originally known as a Girdle Bug, this new variation has taken many Western rivers by storm and has become the fly of choice for numerous float-fishing guides in Colorado and the neighboring states. Tied solely from lead wire, chenille, and Super Floss, this pattern is quick and easy to tie and really does catch more fish than it has a right to. Perhaps its simple construction is what gives it the edge; the pattern's simple chenille body with wriggling antennae, tails, and legs may be all one really needs to catch fish. Actually, it seems to be *exactly* what one needs and then some.

Tied from size 4 down to about a 12, and in colors ranging from black and dark brown to golden orange, the Pat's Rubber Legs is an effective representation of a variety of stonefly nymphs. I haven't found a river yet where it doesn't produce. The float guides on the Colorado River like to use it under a large indicator, often with a smaller *Baetis* or generic searching pattern tethered behind it on a dropper. Fished straight down the center of the river, the guides will glide the boat along the currents, guiding the flies into the most likely looking water and keeping their clients happily securing fish on nearly every drift. Wade anglers fish it much the same way, typically with a bit of additional split shot to keep it plying the substrate, and they are often smiling behind bent rods as well.

As simple as this pattern is, there are a few little tricks to tying it. I can attest that the legs themselves should be tied in deceptively close together. I tie them in with X-wraps and try to place them about two chenille wrap widths apart. Tying them this closely spaced allows you to use the chenille wraps themselves to help separate them and removes some of the frustration from tying this pattern. I've found that Super Floss is the right stuff to use for the legs as well, rather than conventional latex rubber legs or Sili Legs. While both of these material options create a fly that will catch fish, Super Floss is much more durable and doesn't dry-rot as easily. God forbid you are forced to tie more of these things than you have to! And finally, I'll show you how to dress these dang things up a little bit to make them seem more like a real fly and less like a cat toy—and it involves sharp things and fire, so read carefully.

I like to tie my version of Pat's Rubber Legs with a relatively small-diameter lead wire underbody wrapped over the length of the shank to keep the fly level and smooth. Using larger-sized lead on the front end of the hook only makes for a tapered body, and while there is nothing inherently wrong with that in itself, the taper can play a bit of havoc with the chenille wraps near the legs. I try not to tie the fly too heavy and I prefer to keep it a bit on the skinny side, which is easy enough to accomplish by slightly spiraling the chenille wraps—not so much as to leave spaces between, but just enough to keep the fly from thickening up too much. Some tie theirs fatter and with more lead, and sure enough, they work too—so maybe a lot of this is in my head. This fly is so fast and easy to tie, you can certainly tie some each way and decide for yourself; in fact, the best part of this fly is that it is so cheap and easy to tie. You'll never get too upset about losing one (unless it's your last one) and that lets you fish them down deep, near structure, and tight to the banks with more confidence. Try that with a twenty-minute stone!

Though the Pat's Rubber Legs doesn't have all the parts to match the stonefly's anatomy, it must have what the fish find important.

PAT'S RUBBER LEGS (GOLDEN)

Hook: #4-12 Daiichi 2220, TMC 5263, or TMC 5262
Weight: Lead or nonlead .015 inch diameter wire
Thread: Black 8/0 Uni
Tail, Legs, and Antennae: Rusty olive Super Floss
Body: Gold/brown variegated chenille

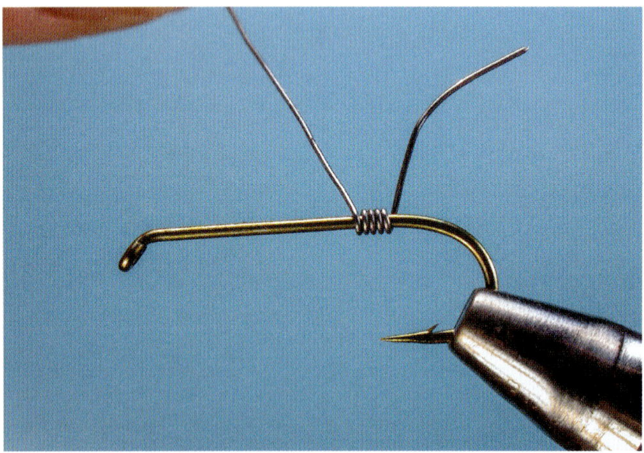

1. Start by mounting the hook in the vise and taking from ten to thirty wraps of lead wire around the hook shank.

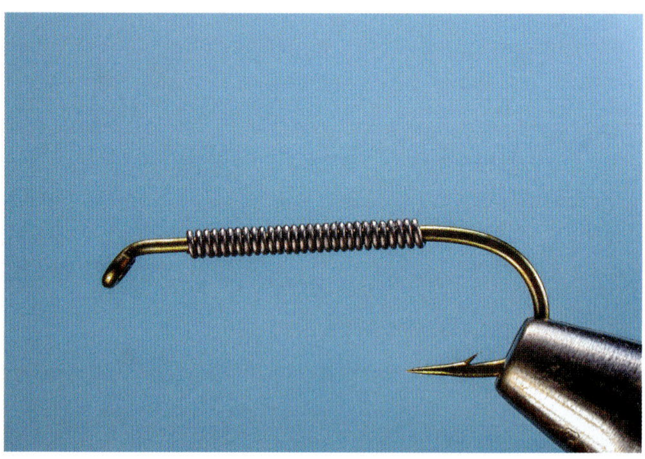

2. Center the lead wraps on the shank. Be sure there is some bare shank on either end of the lead wraps before you start the thread.

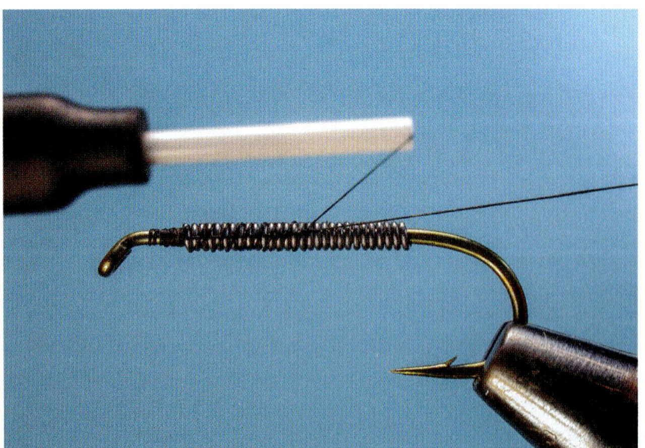

3. Start the thread just behind the hook eye and wrap back to the front of the lead wraps, forming a small thread dam as you build up to the diameter of the lead. Continue wrapping back over the lead wire and the tag end of the thread to the rear of the lead wraps then trim the tag.

4. Build another small thread dam on the rear end of the lead wraps, tapering down to the hook shank. Continue the thread base all the way to the bend of the hook. Wrap the thread forward again to the back of the index point. You can add a drop of head cement to the thread wraps and lead at this point if you're into that kind of thing.

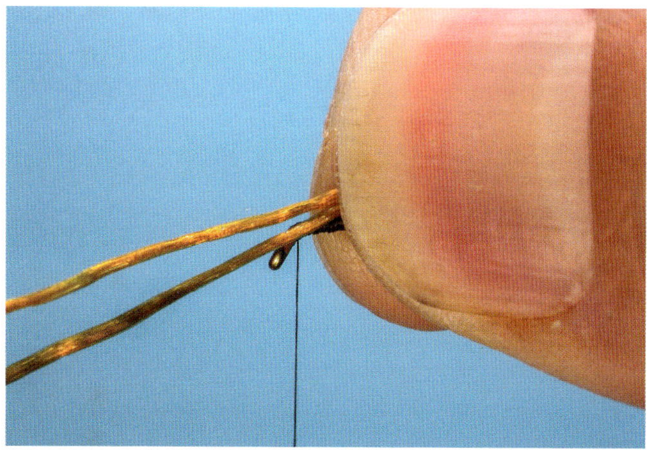

5. Cut two three-inch lengths of Super Floss and pinch them in your fingertips behind the eye of the hook. You should have a little more than a shank length of Super Floss sticking out of your fingers.

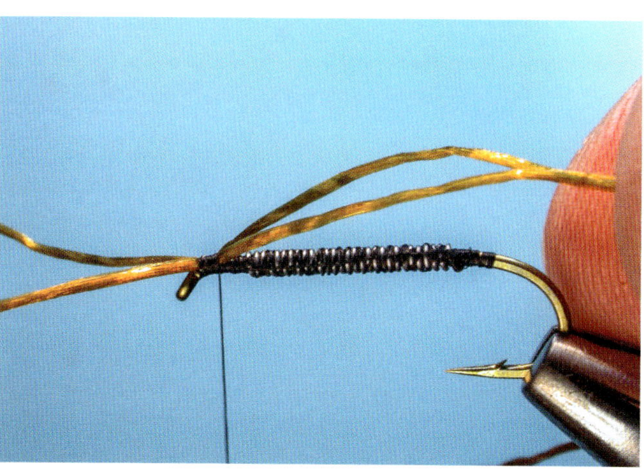

6. Capture the Super Floss with a few tight thread turns to center the two strands on top of the hook behind the eye. Anchor the floss in place with a narrow band of thread.

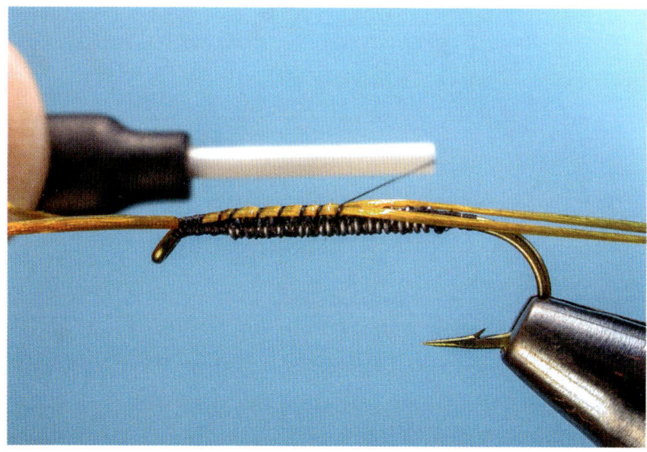

7. Stretch the back two strands of Super Floss toward the bend of the hook and wrap back over the taut strands with evenly spaced turns.

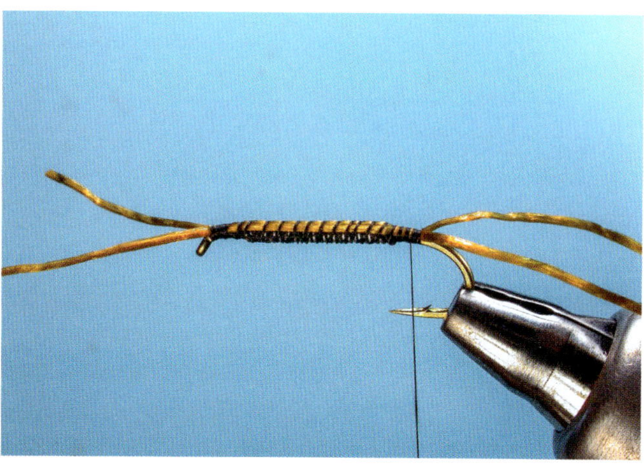

8. Continue wrapping over the Super Floss all the way back to the bend of the hook, where you will again anchor the strands in place with another narrow band of thread. Make sure both the tails and the antennae are centered on the hook. If they're crooked the fish will laugh.

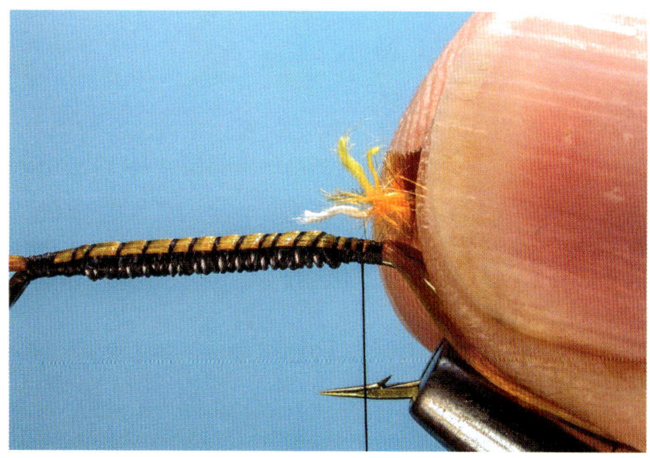

9. Leave the thread hanging at the bend and cut a length of chenille for the body. Peel the fibers from one end of the chenille, exposing the thread core.

10. Catch the thread core of the chenille with a few turns of thread right at the bend. Tying the chenille in by just the core will prevent bulk from building up at the bend and making a lump in the body.

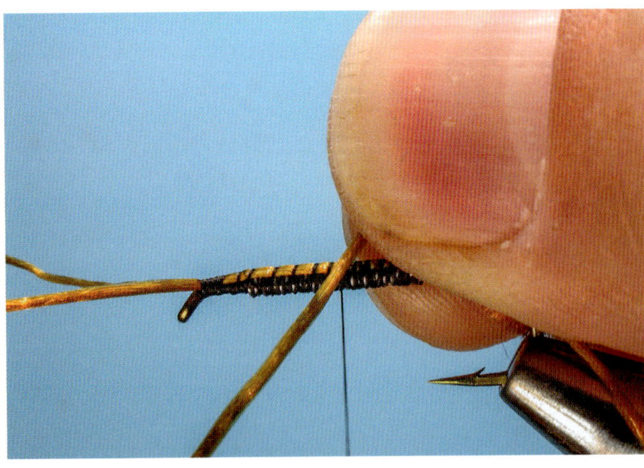

11. Move the thread forward to just ever so slightly in front of the halfway point. Cut a two-inch length of Super Floss and lay it across the hook at a right angle.

12. Make two stacked diagonal wraps over the Super Floss at the center of its length. These first two wraps should be right on top of each other and go from the near side of the hook on the back side of the strand to the far side of the hook on the front side of the strand.

13. Now make two more stacked diagonal wraps, this time at the opposite angle. These next two wraps should go from the front side of the near strand to the back side of the far strand. You are making a simple set of X-wraps here. Be sure to keep the wraps perfectly stacked to prop the strand perpendicular to the hook.

14. Move the thread forward a little less than half the distance between the first leg and the hook eye.

15. Tie in the second set of legs as you did the first, then move the thread forward again for the third set. The placement here can be a bit tricky, but basically you want enough room in front of the front set of legs to make two wraps of chenille. You can see the legs are pretty much an equal distance apart. Do your own math and make yours look like this.

16. Begin wrapping the chenille in tight, abutting turns right in front of the base of the tail. Continue wrapping forward to the back of the first set of legs. If this wrap doesn't line up just right against the back of the first set of legs, that's totally cool and maybe a little fortuitous.

17. Draw the near-side leg rearward and make a half turn of chenille right up against its front edge. This wrap ought to hold the Super Floss leg at a slightly rearward angle. See? Fortuitous!

18. Continue that same turn of chenille over the top of the hook and pull the far-side leg to the back of the hook as you pin it in place with the rest of the wrap of chenille. You are using the chenille itself to position the legs

19. Make one more complete turn of chenille between the first and second sets of legs, then repeat the process to work the chenille around the second set of legs.

20. Finally, draw the front set of legs back and make a wrap tight up to their front edge with the chenille. Make one more turn of chenille up to the back of the index point.

21. Lift the chenille up and tie it off with a few tight turns of thread.

22. Clip the excess chenille as closely as you can, then go back and trim any of the fluff from the chenille that may have gotten caught in the tie-down.

23. Chenille generally makes for a pretty bulky tie-off, so take the extra few seconds to clean up the head area before continuing. Build a smooth thread head over the butt end of the chenille and then whip-finish and clip the thread.

24. Grab all three legs on each side in each hand and stretch them a bit while you tweak them to square on the hook.

25. Lift all the legs above the shank without stretching them and clip them straight across at about a half shank length. You may need to even things up a bit individually, which is fine.

26. Trim the antennae to just slightly shorter than a shank length and the tails to right at a shank length.

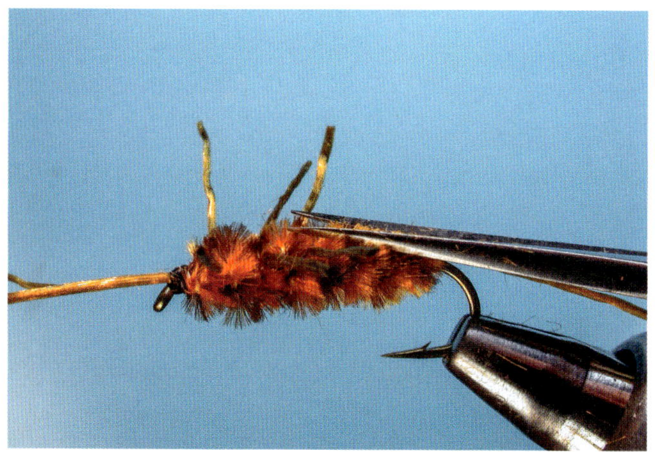

27. Now, you could fish this fly just as it is and catch piles of fish, and some of you will surely elect to do just that, but my natural proclivity to dress things up a bit takes over here. Use your scissors to taper the chenille at the back of the hook a bit by trimming the fluff at an angle. This slight taper really makes no difference to the fish—but it makes me feel a lot better about fishing this dumb thing, so I do it every time.

Continue shaping the body a bit so that instead of a thick turd-shaped fly, you have a bit more of a cigar or club shape. I also trim a bit of the fluff along the front of the fly in order to taper it back down toward the hook eye.

28. Grab all the legs and the tails in one hand and pull them down under the shank. Use a cigarette lighter to singe the chenille a little to clean up the taper. It's a small detail, but your Pat's Rubber Legs will look way better than the ones your buddies fish with, and therefore will catch the smarter fish.

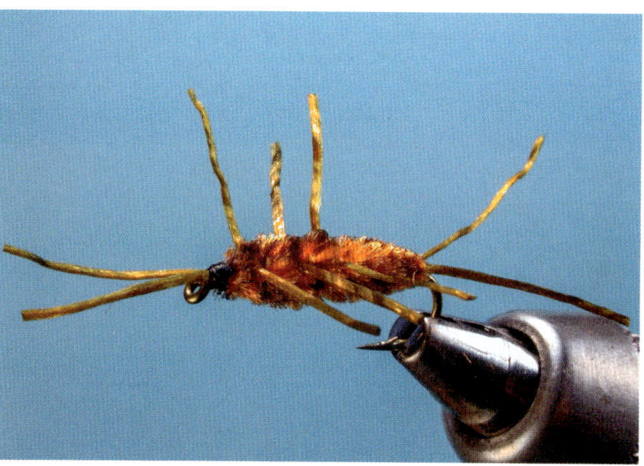

29. You can't say the tapered body doesn't improve the looks of this fly. You can't. Add a drop of head cement to the thread head.

13

RUBBER-LEG HARE'S EAR

Adding just a few accoutrements from other popular flies to the venerable Hare's Ear makes for a much more compelling and specific pattern. The technique used for adding the Super Floss legs to a dubbed thorax is easily converted to other patterns, and the Clear Cure Goo coated wingcase adds depth, weight, and durability.

While you can probably see right off the bat that this version is really just a dressed-up account of one of the most popular and effective nymphs of all time, I urge you to look a bit closer. I have always been a big fan of rubber legs on patterns in the #10-14 range (where appropriate), and the Hare's Ear lends itself wonderfully to these parameters. These sizes fall in line with a variety of small- to medium-sized stonefly nymphs as well as some of the larger mayfly nymphs like Green Drakes, all of which have fairly prominent legs and share a similar profile. The version I'll tie here is meant to imitate a smaller Golden Stonefly nymph, but obviously it can be tied in a range of colors. Notice that

Like the original Hare's Ear, this is a real workhorse pattern. You can tie it large for stoneflies and in medium sizes it is an excellent large mayfly nymph pattern. Tied in olive it is a good match for the robust Western Green Drake nymphs.

while I reference this pattern as a "rubber leg" version, I do not use the traditional latex rubber strands for the legs but rather Super Floss, a spandex elastic that is far less prone to dry-rotting, is way more durable, and comes in a huge range of colors. Of course you can use conventional rubber leg materials on yours, but don't gripe about it when the legs dry up and fall off in a year. One of the added advantages of the Super Floss is that it can be easily split into smaller strands using the tip of a dubbing needle, so legs of the appropriate diameter for nearly any size fly can be fashioned right at your tying bench.

One of the best tricks I'll show you for making this fly was unabashedly stolen from my friend John Barr. The method he uses to install the rubber legs on his Rubber Leg Copper John is both ingenious and nearly foolproof. I remember getting orders for RLHEs when I was a kid and fighting to position the dang rubber legs on every one of them. Man, I hated this fly! Then, several years ago, John asked me to tie, photograph, and write the tutorials for his book *Barr Flies*. Of course I jumped at the chance and worked closely with John for several months to re-create his patterns true to John's original versions. In that time I picked up a ton of great little tips—the simple way he attached the legs on his Rubber Leg Copper John among them. I know I go on and on about JB all the time in my writing, but there are few tiers who have such a clean, uncluttered view of tying as John and he has some of the best ideas I've ever heard. If you haven't bought his book yet, you should do that right now. I'll give you a minute.

The rest of the pattern is pretty true to the original Gold-Ribbed Hare's Ear, but I couldn't resist dressing it up a bit. I coat the turkey quill wing case with a drop of Clear Cure Goo for starters. The coating toughens up the wing case, brightens things up a bit, and adds a little weight. Clear Cure Goo is my choice of the modern UV set polymers that are replacing conventional five-minute epoxy in the fly tying world. About the same viscosity as normal two part epoxy, the Tack Free Brushable version of CCG is easily applied and cures instantly when a UV light is applied. This stuff is so much easier and less messy than epoxy, I find myself using it in places where I would never have previously considered using a coating. In this case, the prospect of coating the wingcase and *waiting for it to dry* before dubbing the neck behind the bead makes epoxy a no-go, but with CCG, it's a no brainer. This also makes the addition of a strip of flash down the middle of the wing case possible and a lot more durable.

This pattern highlights a few bells and whistles that can be added to any nymph pattern. The heavy tungsten bead, wriggling set of rubber legs, UV-coated wing case, and a little color change helps create something that looks familiar but oh-so-much more interesting and fishable! Let this fly spark a bit of creative thinking on your part. It's stuff like this that makes fly tying so fun, and this "Mr. Potato Head" aspect of mixing and matching this part and that can often generate new ideas and even patterns.

RUBBER-LEG HARE'S EAR

Hook: #8-16 TMC 5262
Thread: Wood duck 70-denier UTC
Bead: Gold tungsten
Weight: Lead wire
Tail: Coq de Leon hen saddle dyed copper olive
Rib: Hot yellow or gold UTC wire (small)
Abdomen: Dyed gold hare's mask dubbing from the cheeks
Wing case: Cinnamon-tipped turkey tail feather slip
Thorax: Dyed gold hare's mask dubbing from the poll
Legs: Amber Super Floss
Coating: Clear Cure Goo, tack-free brushable UV polymer
Neck: Same as thorax

BEAD TO HOOK SIZE

1.5 mm (1/16")	#22-24
2 mm (5/64")	#18-20
2.3 mm (3/32")	#14-16
2.7 mm (7/64")	#12-14
3.25 mm (1/8")	#10-12
3.8 mm (5/32")	#8-10
4.7 mm (3/16")	#6-8

LEAD WIRE TO HOOK SIZE

.010" diameter	#16-20
.015" diameter	#14-16
.020" diameter	#12-14
.025" diameter	#8-10
.030" diameter	#6-8
.035" diameter	#2-4

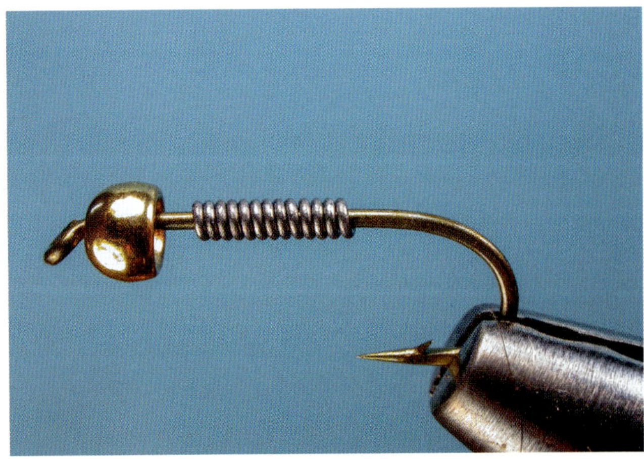

1. Place the bead on the hook and slide it up to the eye. Make about a dozen wraps of lead wire around the shank and break off the stub ends.

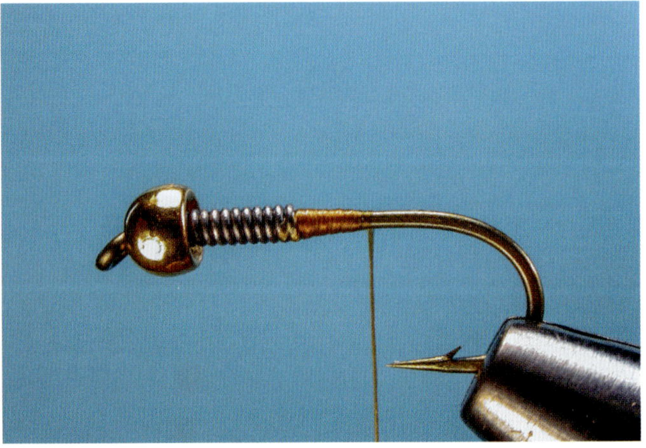

2. Push the lead up into the back of the bead, recessing it into the hole. Start the tying thread right behind the lead wraps on the bare shank. Begin building a thread dam at the rear of the lead wraps, tapering up from the bare shank to the lead.

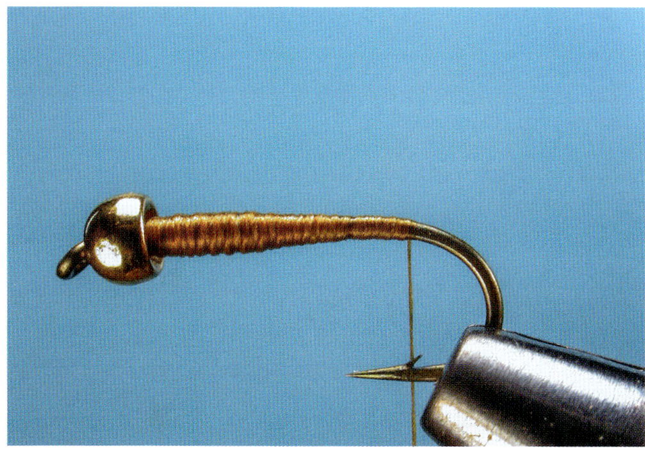

3. Continue building the thread dam until it reaches the diameter of the lead, then keep wrapping forward over the lead wraps to the back of the bead. Work all the way back to the bend again, forming a smoothly tapered thread underbody. Depending on the hook size used, you may need to make a few passes to form this shape.

4. Select a hen feather and preen a small bunch of fibers out from the stem so their tips are even. Peel this clump from the stem and fold it into a bundle. Measure this bundle against the shank so it is a little more than a half shank in length. Tie the tail in at the bend with a tight, narrow band of thread right on top of the hook.

5. Wrap forward over the remaining butt ends to just short of the bead and clip the excess.

6. Tie in a length of wire at the 75 percent point.

7. Lay the wire in along the side of the shank and wrap the thread back over it to the base of the tail. Once at the bend, make a narrow band of thread to anchor it.

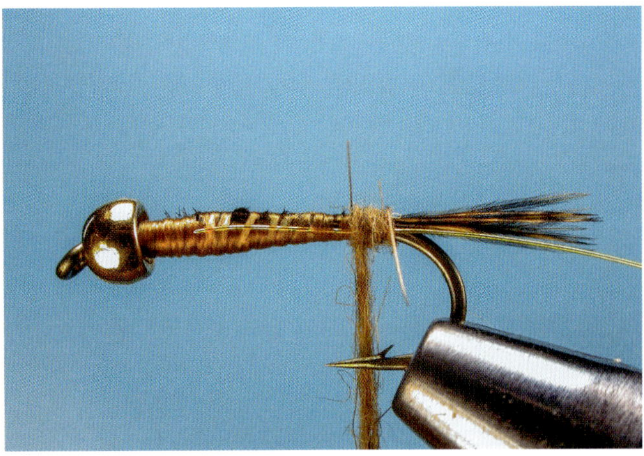

8. Dub a thin strand of the soft fur from the cheek of the hare's mask. Start this dubbing with the first turn at the bend of the hook right at the base of the tail.

9. Build a tapered abdomen as you wrap forward with the dubbing up to the 75 percent point. There is not much overlap of the dubbing necessary because the underbody was well tapered to begin with.

10. This is one of the only patterns that I tie with a counter-wound rib as I feel it makes the ribbing and segmentation a bit more prominent. Be sure to wrap with evenly spaced turns to the front of the abdomen.

11. Once to the front of the abdomen, pull down hard on the wire and cross it with the thread several times, taking care that the thread torque doesn't push the wire end back and loosen it. Helicopter the end of the wire to break it off.

12. Overlap the thread onto the front of the abdomen back to the 60 percent point. Make a small band of thread at this point.

13. Cut a slip from a turkey tail feather that has a tip that is about as wide as the gap of the hook. Trim the ragged tips from the feather slip, leaving a square-cut end.

14. Place the square-cut tip end of the turkey slip on top of the abdomen at the 60 percent point with the inside of the feather slip facing up. Make sure the tip doesn't quite reach the bead. Place your thumb on top of the slip to hold it flat across the top of the shank.

15. Capture the tip of the slip with a few turns of thread, anchoring it flat across the top of the abdomen.

16. Wrap forward over the remaining tips to the back of the bead, smoothing off the thorax area as you go.

17. Dub the thread again, this time with the darker and coarser fur from the center (poll) of the hare's mask. Start this dubbing at the back edge of the bead and work back to the base of the wing case.

18. Work the dubbing into a rectangular thorax shape and end with bare thread hanging in the center of the thorax area on top of the dubbing.

19. Clip a two-inch length of Super Floss and lay it along the far side of the hook with the center of its length even with the thread band in the center of the thorax. Tie the Super Floss strand in right on top of the dubbing with a few turns of thread, taking care to keep it centered along the far side of the thorax.

20. Tie in another two-inch length of Super Floss along the near side of the thorax, and make a wider band of thread here to help separate the legs.

21. Apply more of the darker dubbing to the thread and use it to cover the leg tie-down area and build the thorax into a more rounded shape.

22. Complete the thorax and finish with bare thread right behind the bead. The thorax should be just slightly over-dubbed here, a bit bigger than usual.

23. Pull the wing case forward over the top of the thorax, taking pains to keep it flat and wide across the top of the dubbing. Hold the long end of the wing case in your thread hand and make a turn of thread over it with your material hand. Pull straight down on the thread to anchor the wing case directly across the top of the thorax. Make certain the wing case is centered and wide enough to encompass the top of the thorax.

24. Make a few more tight turns of thread to secure the wing case and then clip the excess flush.

25. Pinch the thorax and wing case down tightly between your fingertips to flatten it a bit.

26. Apply a drop of Clear Cure Goo Tack Free to the wing case. Make sure to cover it edge to edge and front to back, with enough CCG to create a slight hump. I like to use a single larger-sized drop to do this rather than applying a thin coat followed by a thicker coat. If you let the CCG sit on the wing case for just a few seconds before cooking it with the UV lamp, it will soak down into and become one with the wing case, making for a bulletproof fly.

27. Cook the CCG with a UV Pro Plus Lamp for about ten seconds to set the goo. Hold the lamp as close as you can to ensure a hard shell.

28. Now, dub just a tiny bit more of the darker dubbing onto the thread and build a small neck behind the bead to cover the tie-off area. You may need to sweep the front legs back and out of your way as you do this.

29. This band of dubbing should be tight and narrow between the back of the bead and the front of the wing case. Whip-finish right on the back edge of the bead and let the thread turns slide off the bead and down in front of the dubbed neck area. Clip the thread.

30. Trim the legs. I pull the back legs back and trim them even with the outside of the hook bend and then trim the front legs just slightly shorter.

31. Pick out the dubbing with your piece of Velcro and sweep it back along the thorax as well as the dubbed neck. We overdubbed this section on purpose, as this roughing process will surely pull a bit of the dubbing out.

32. That's a pretty buggy, simple-to-tie fly right there. Other colors? Brown, black, and even olive lend themselves nicely to this pattern.

Golden Stones thrive in many rivers throughout the country and good imitations of them should be a staple in your fly box. Colorado's South Platte River (above) has dense populations of Golden Stoneflies and fishing one is almost always a good option in faster water.

14

SOFT-HACKLE

Like so many great patterns, Soft-Hackles are simple to tie, but keeping them sparse and slim is paramount. Building a smooth floss body and building experience with game bird feather collars are just a couple of things this fly will teach you.

I use folded soft-hackle collars on an awful lot of my flies. Even when a pattern is typically tied with a normal hen hackle feather collar, I still almost always fold the feather to sweep it back in a more graceful way. I'm not sure when I started doing this but I can imagine that it was shortly after I figured out how to do it. The folded-hackle technique results in such a beautiful, swept-back collar that I find it hard to resist from an aesthetic point of view as well as an ease-of-tying perspective. Folded feathers are easier to wrap cleanly and tend not to trap and catch errant fibers, as often happens with an unfolded feather. To that end, I will use the simple Soft-Hackle fly design here to highlight the proper technique for folding a soft-hackle feather, whether it comes from a hen, rooster, or game bird. This technique is a valuable arrow in your quiver that you'll likely find yourself using increasingly often.

I see more and more anglers fishing these old-school patterns these days, and the current fish love them just as much as their forerunners did back in the day. The patterns' inherent movement and sparseness makes them imitative of a variety of insects without being too specific and getting pigeonholed. Typically fished with no weight on a soft rod and swung across the current to let the hackle dance and move, Soft-Hackles are particularly good imitations of emerging caddis pupae. I have fished long enough to know that while I really like to call my shot and tie specific patterns to imitate specific bugs, I will still end the day pretty happy if I have a bunch of fish to my credit even in cases where I don't know exactly why they ate the fly. It gives me something to think about on the drive home.

The traditional Soft-Hackle pattern presents a good opportunity for tiers to gain an appreciation for sparseness in material use and design. Popularized by Sylvester Nemes, Soft-Hackles are simple to tie and are incredibly effective on all water types. Today their construction can vary from slender and sparse to brusque and burly, but it is the sparsely dressed, floss-bodied version that comes first to mind when the phrase "soft-hackled fly" is heard. While commonly tied using Pearsall's Silk Thread, a more compact form of silk, I prefer to use silk floss instead, as the body just looks so much prettier. If you opt to use the thread, the fly becomes even more simple, although somewhat limited to larger-sized flies because the thread has a bigger diameter than most conventional tying threads.

Silk floss is not a material that is used often enough these days and it can be a little intimidating, so I decided to use it here to demonstrate a couple techniques. It's not the easiest material to work with and does require a bit of know-how to work properly, and I intend on explaining the tips as best I can.

Silk floss is unique in that when wet, it lets the color of the underlying thread show through and influence the overall tone of the floss itself. To that end, many tiers opt to use lighter-colored or white thread under floss bodies to maintain the desired coloration of their flies. Some of the real smart guys out there use complementary tones under the floss to change the overall shade of the pattern as well. Yellow thread under gray floss makes a beautiful olive color, black thread under white floss makes a nice gray, and red under yellow will give you an orange tone—pretty crafty, if you ask me, and it opens up a whole plethora of color variations.

There's not really much to these flies beyond the floss and soft-hackle feather collar, just a small dubbed thorax designed to prop the collar up a bit and add a hint of bugginess, but this simple fly presents a range of new tying techniques to even the experienced tier. Heck, I'll even show you an alternative method to use when you can't find partridge feathers that are small enough for the tiny hooks.

Buy a whole Hungarian partridge hide rather than a bag of assorted body feathers. You'll get many more useable feathers and have the luxury of picking individual feathers from the hide instead of hunting through a bag of fluff for the right one.

SOFT-HACKLE

Hook: #12-18 TMC 3769
Thread: Black (or tier's color of choice) 16/0 Veevus
Abdomen: Gold silk floss
Thorax: Nearly any type of natural fur dubbing; hare's mask was used here
Hackle: Hungarian partridge body feather

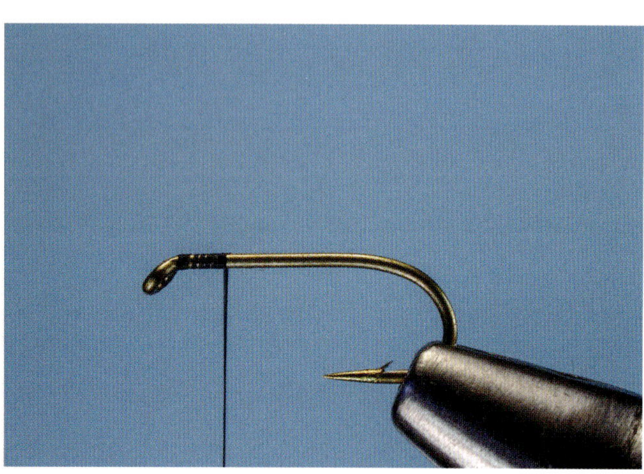

1. Attach the thread just behind the eye and wrap back about two eye lengths.

2. Cut a six-inch length of floss from the spool and begin to split it by twisting the ends in your fingertips in opposite directions. Once unfurled a bit, the floss will separate into several strands. Grab the separated floss at the center of its length and gently pull it apart, from the middle to the ends, into smaller strands.

3. For a size 12 fly, I'll usually use about three of these smaller strands. Once you separate the strands they tend to twist back up on themselves to form nice and tight smaller strands that are easy to use.

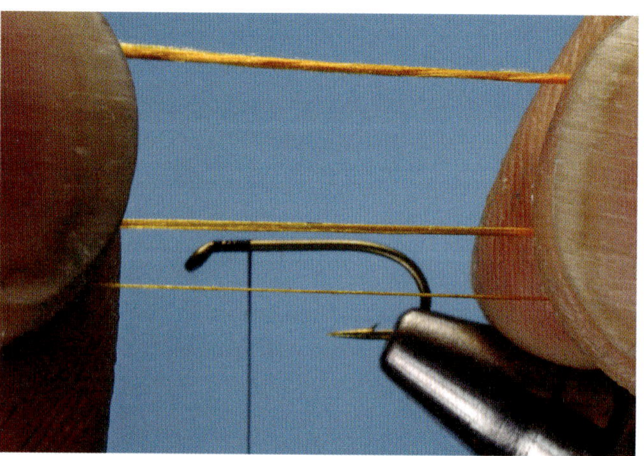

4. For illustrative purposes, here is a whole, un-split strand of floss on top, the three smaller strands we will use on this size 12 fly in the center, and a single strand at the bottom. For smaller or more sparsely dressed patterns, a single strand is often all that is needed and helps to ensure a smooth, seamless body.

5. Grasp the three strands by their ends in one hand and run your fingers down their length several times to flatten the strands and remove the twist before tying it in and align the fibers so there is no slack in the strand. Be sure your hands are clean and de-burred (use an emery board to sand rough spots off your fingers) before doing this so you don't discolor light-colored floss or fray the fibers.

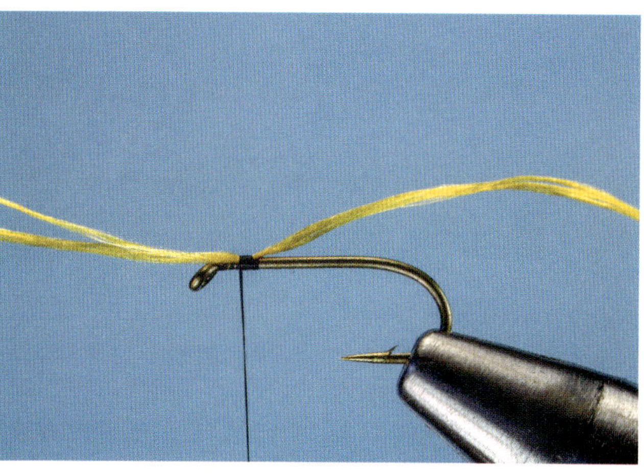

6. Tie in the floss about two eye lengths back from the hook eye using exactly four turns of thread in a tight, narrow band.

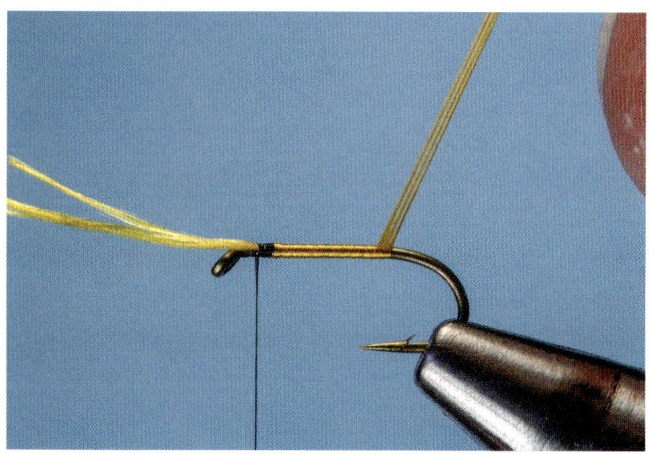

7. Begin wrapping the floss as smoothly as you can to a point back between the point on the hook and the point on the barb. This first layer must be as smooth as possible. Note that the floss is lying flat and wide here, rather than corded up.

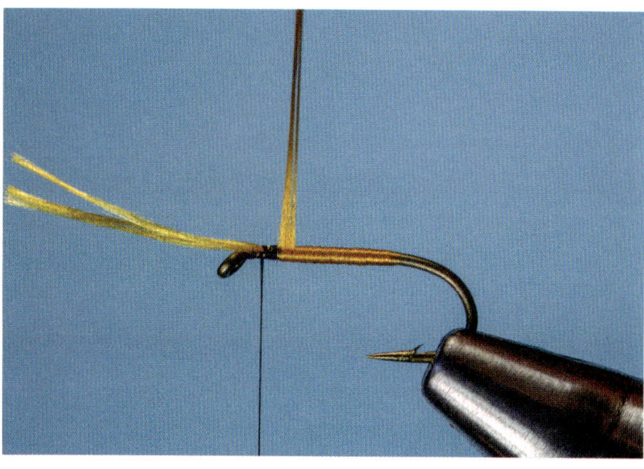

8. Wrap the floss forward again over the first layer, again taking pains to keep it as smooth as you can. You can, at your discretion, overlap the floss a bit on this second trip to build a slight taper; both level and tapered bodies catch fish and look great when done well.

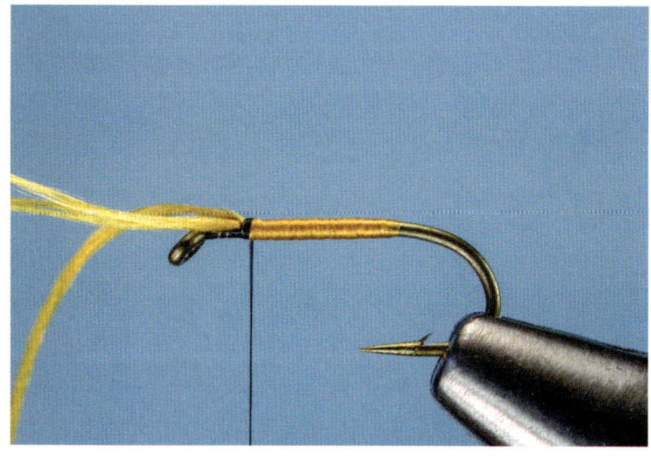

9. Before tying off the floss, unwrap three of the turns of thread you used to tie the floss in. Removing these three turns will cut down on bulk and essentially allow you to tie the floss both in and off with the same four turns of thread. It's not a huge deal on a bigger fly like this but you can see where this technique will helpful on smaller, more sparsely dressed patterns or wherever bulk becomes an issue.

10. Clip the stub ends of the floss flush to the hook and make a turn or two of thread over what's left. Use a smooth metal or glass rod to burnish the body and smooth it out by rubbing the tool firmly up and down all sides of the floss body. There are specific burnishing tools sold for this purpose but I have always used the smooth handle of my dubbing brush, the rounded outside edge of my scissors, or even the side of a thick bodkin needle.

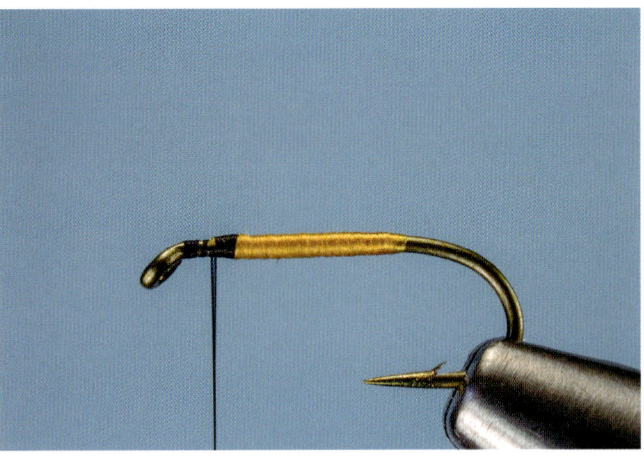

11. Here's a little closer look at the burnished body. You can see the floss has been smoothed out considerably. I'm certain fish will eat the fly without this step, although when it's this easy to do it right, there's little reason to omit it.

12. Dub a thin strand of dubbing onto the thread and wrap it to form a ball at the front of the floss abdomen. Leave about an eye length of hook exposed in front of the thorax. Nearly any natural dubbing can be used here, typically something a little buggy. I have used natural hare's mask dubbing from the poll here, but beaver, mole, muskrat, and plain old rabbit fur all work beautifully as well. Make certain at this point that there is a thread base on the shank between the front of the thorax and the hook eye if there is not one there already. We want to be sure to tie the upcoming hackle feather in on top of a thread base and not onto bare shank.

13. Select a partridge feather from the hide that has barbs equal to about a shank length. Peel the fluff and stray fibers from the base of the feather, leaving only the bare stem exposed. Stroke the feather fibers back toward the base of the feather while holding on to the tip of the feather; it should leave you with something that looks like this.

14. Lay the feather in on top of the hook. Tie it in at the front of the thorax by the tip at the point at which the fibers are stroked back and the fibers in the tip separate. Be sure to anchor the feather down tightly here; we are about to pull and tug on it a bit and accidentally pulling the feather out will require starting over with a new one. It will also include a few words your mother told you not to say.

15. Clip the excess tip of the feather as close as you can to the hook and make a couple more turns of thread over the stub to further anchor it. Leave the thread hanging right at the back of the hook eye. Make sure the inside concave face of the feather is facing the hook shank.

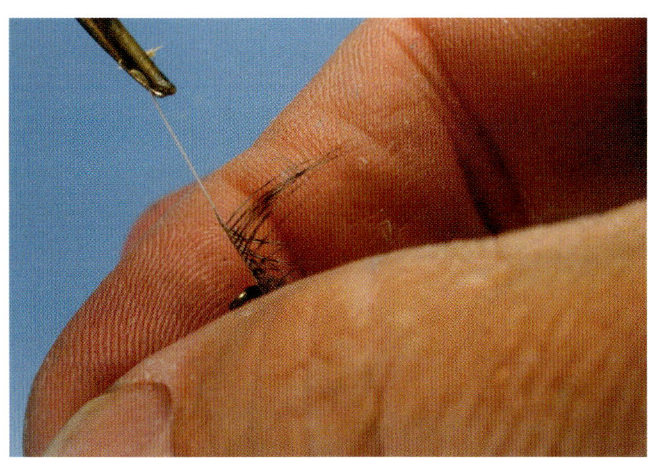

16. Grab the tip of the bare stem (actually the butt end of the feather) in your hackle pliers and lift the feather straight up above the shank with the inside of the feather facing the hook bend. Wet the tip of your thumb and index finger on your material hand while holding the hackle pliers with your thread hand. Bring your fingers around the front of the feather and pinch them together. At this point you are making an "O" with your thumb and index finger around the feather. In this photo I have dropped my "O" a bit so you can see that the feather is inside, but you'll want to keep the closed part of your fingertips above the hook shank for this step.

17. Now, simultaneously slide the closed tips of your "O" fingers back over the feather as you pull forward on the hackle pliers to fold the feather fibers back to one side of the stem. When viewed from the top, the fibers should form a "V" with the stem of the feather in the narrow end and the fibers forming the legs. Work your "O" fingers up and down a bit to firmly crease the fibers in place. You may need to repeat this step a couple times to get a good clean fold, so don't get impatient. A properly folded hackle wraps beautifully and results in a great-looking fly.

18. We now have a nicely folded feather. Soft feathers like partridge don't crease quite as well as stiffer feathers like hen or rooster saddle; nonetheless, folding the feather makes for a cleaner wrap and prettier collar.

19. Repeat the "O" process one more time, but on this go-round you should begin wrapping the feather over the hook with the hackle pliers while you hold the folded fibers back along the shank.

20. Here's about a half turn into the first wrap. You can see the hackle fibers slope gently back toward the bend as a result of the folding process. Continue wrapping to complete the turn and perhaps add one more, but no more than that. Soft-Hackles should be tied quite sparsely and one turn of hackle is typically just right.

21. Complete that first turn and tie the feather off just behind the hook eye with a couple tight turns of thread. You should be tying off over just the bare stem of the feather, not over any remaining hackle fibers. Clip the excess stem flush and build a smooth thread head, then whip-finish and clip the thread.

22. Our finished Soft-Hackle. Splitting the floss allows for beautifully slim bodies on even the smallest patterns and helps emphasize the utility of sparseness.

23. Front view; note the sparse hackle.

TYING SMALL SOFT-HACKLES

One of the problems inherent in using partridge feathers for soft-hackled flies is the difficulty in finding feathers small enough for flies size 16 and smaller. Here is an alternative method of hackling for smaller flies.

1. Build the abdomen and thorax as you normally would, but perhaps with just a single strand of floss for the body to keep it thin on this smaller hook.

2. Select a partridge feather that has a square-shaped end with just slight rounding on the edges, if any.

3. Peel all the fluff and longer fibers from the base of the feather while holding the square tips firmly in your fingertips. This should leave you with a triangle-shaped feather tip similar to that seen here.

4. Use the tips of your scissors to clip out the center stem toward the tip of the feather. You want fibers that are more than long enough to reach the hook bend here, and a clean "V" shape in the feather.

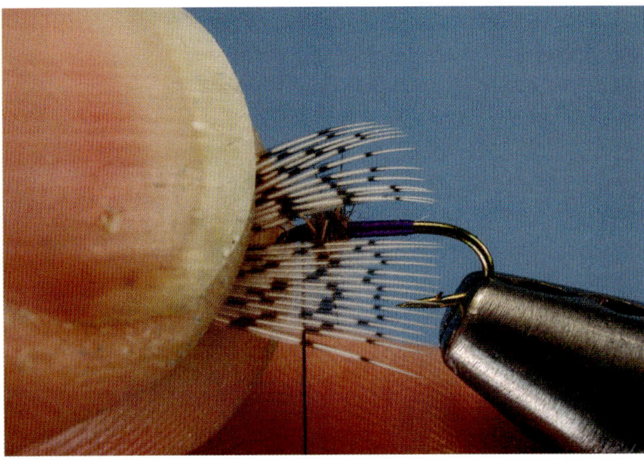

5. Lay the feather atop the hook with the base of the "V" well in front of the hook eye and each side of the "V" on either side of the hook shank. The tips of the feather fibers should reach back to about the point on the barb.

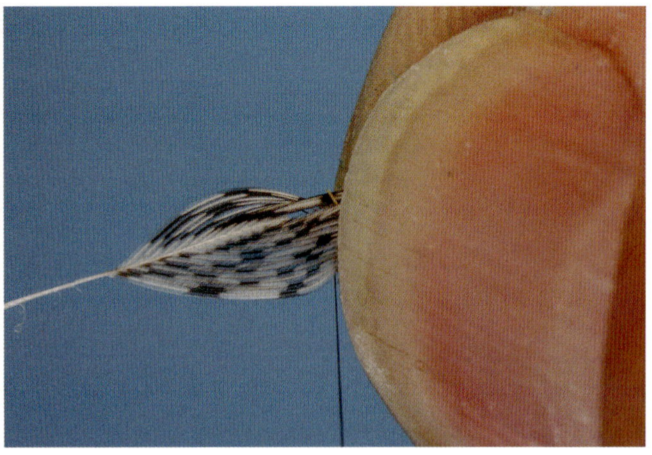

6. Bring your material hand in from the back of the vise and pinch the two sides of the "V" down along the sides of the hook, trying to keep them flat and in a sheet on each side. Think of a tent shape across the top of the fly.

7. Make two loose turns of thread around the base of the feather in front of your fingertips and then tighten the thread by drawing it toward you. You should loosen your grasp on the tips just slightly as you tighten the thread; you'll feel the fibers roll slightly in your fingertips.

8. You should have a somewhat fully splayed hackle collar. Make another couple turns of thread and let these wraps further distribute the fibers around the shank. Often the fibers won't roll all the way around to the bottom of the shank. If they are all bunched up in one spot, manually distribute them with your fingers if need be. The collar does not have to go all the way around; there are plenty of fibers to provide the needed movement and the fish will never know better.

9. Come in with the tips of your finest scissors and clip the excess butt ends of the feather flush against the hook shank behind the eye. Build a smooth thread head over the butt ends and whip-finish. I don't like head cement on any of my soft-hackled flies because it tends to bleed up into the hackle and stiffen it, but do whatever you're comfortable with. I'm not your mom.

10. Finished fly.

You can tie Soft-Hackles in just about any color combination. Though floss and partridge are traditional choices for these flies, experiment with different body materials and feathers.

15

FRENCHIE

Jig hooks have been used for years in conventional fishing but have only caught on recently in the fly fishing world. The right angle hook eye position forces the fly to ride hook point up and keeps even the heaviest flies more snag free than when tied on conventional hooks.

Regardless of how you or I might feel about competitive fly fishing, there is no arguing that it has brought a ton of innovation in technique and fly patterns to our sport. Charging passionate and highly talented anglers and fly tiers with the sole purpose of catching as many fish as possible has fostered not only some incredibly effective fishing techniques, but also a host of new purpose-driven and well-designed fly patterns.

As you might guess, the Frenchie is a product of the French competitive team, and it's one of the easiest-to-tie patterns in this book. Don't let the ease of tying sway your thoughts on how effective and well put-together this fly really is though. Design elements that were hardly considered until recently shine through on this simple fly. A sparse tail of mottled Coq de Leon fibers, a slim, compact abdomen of turkey or pheasant tail fibers ribbed with copper wire, and a tightly dubbed hot spot behind a bead head are all the it takes to build this wonderful little fly, but the way in which they are put together and the innovative design makes for a fly that is easy to tie, durable, and sinks like a stone. Originally tied on a conventional nymph hook, the Frenchie has more

The Frenchie and its variations exploit a "hot spot" of bright thread or dubbing around the collar of the fly.

recently been transferred to a jig hook chassis, allowing the fly to drag right along the bottom and ride hook point-up, keeping it relatively snag-free and positioned to hook fish at the slightest provocation.

While the conventional method of making a fly sink well involves tungsten beads and copious amounts of lead wire, there is another element to a fly pattern's sink rate that is often overlooked. Flies that are tied slim and sparse, yet still heavy, will sink faster than bulkier, shaggier flies of the same physical weight simply because they cut through the water more easily without any "appendages" to hold them up. Think of a skydiving free fall: the parachutist folds in his arms and legs and plummets through the air at an amazing rate, then opens the chute and slows his descent dramatically.

What slows down the skydiver is the same property that makes a dry fly float well and also what keeps a nymph from sinking well: surface area. A slim fly tied with a compact profile will sink more quickly than an identically weighted fly tied more full, robustly, or shaggy. John Barr's incredibly effective Slumpbuster streamer pattern is a shining example of this concept: It has a thin profile, good weight, and great sink rate. Fly tying can be so much more than lashing a few materials to a hook and calling it good. When done well, flies are not just well tied, but well designed with their intended purpose in mind. The Frenchie is a perfect small attractor nymph designed to look a little like a lot of different food sources, but more importantly, it's meant to plummet to the bottom of the river and stay there. This is a good lesson to keep in mind as you tie and fish various patterns. Think not only of imitating a generic or specific food source, but how you can go about obtaining a specific sink rate.

While the conventional Frenchie is a cinch to tie, adapting it to a jig hook adds just a couple small considerations to the tying process. Jig hooks, with the eye on an upright section of shank at 60 to 90 degrees to the main hook shank, require the use of a slotted tungsten bead rather than a conventional counter-drilled bead. The slot allows the bead to seat up against the upright at the front of the hook and positions the bead so that it alters the way the hook rides. Slotted beads are available in all the regular sizes and colors and can often be found in the plain, smooth, round versions as well as in faceted varieties with a bit of added texture. I'm not sure that any of this particular detail really makes any difference to the fish, but the faceted beads certainly add a flair of out-of-the-ordinary to this simple fly. I have found that I like to slightly oversize the bead on these flies to make them even heavier, and the jig hook makes this possible without completely throwing off the proportions of the fly.

The hot spot at the head of this fly has become a staple of many European-style nymphs, and while this example is tied with red thread and a pink dubbed hotspot, feel free to substitute other colors. Orange, red, pink, and yellow hot spots all add a bit of an attractor flair, while a more subtle head of rough natural hare's mask or darker rabbit fur can be more imitative.

FRENCHIE

Hook: #12-18 TMC 400BLJ
Bead: Copper or black slotted faceted tungsten
Thread: Red 8/0 Uni
Tail: Medium Coq de Leon (CDL) fibers
Rib: Copper UTC Wire (small)
Abdomen: Natural turkey tail fibers or pheasant tail
Thorax: Hot pink Ice Dub

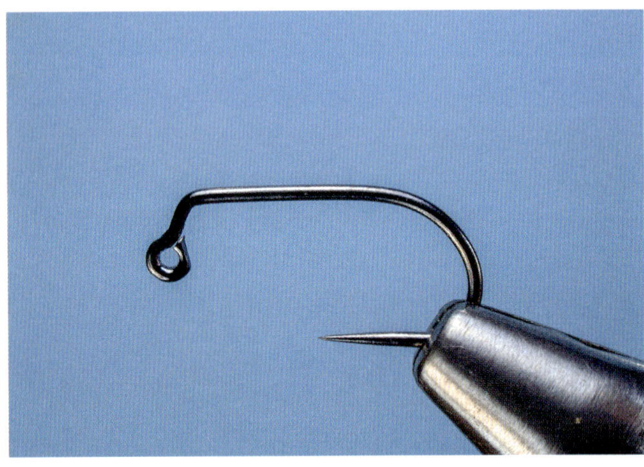

1. This is a Tiemco jig-style competition hook. The eye is canted upward and in line with the shank and the hook point is extended slightly longer than ordinary. Because it is barbless, the long point helps it hold better; in competitions, a long point is the next best thing to a barbed hook.

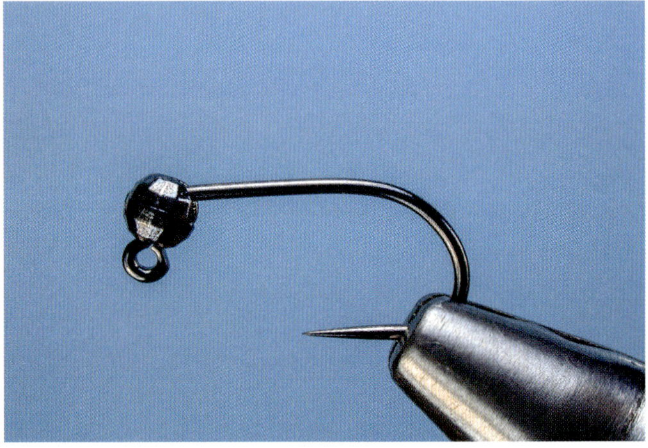

2. Slide the slotted bead onto the hook and up to the eye. Jig hooks require a slotted bead—rather than conically drilled conventional bead—in order to fit on the upright section of the hook at the eye. Make sure you have the right thing on here or else it's not going to work.

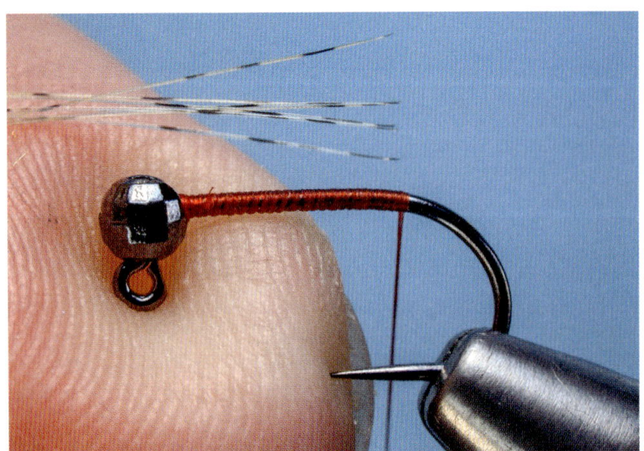

3. Start the thread right behind the bead and wrap a thread base back to the hook bend. Select a CDL feather and preen the fibers so the tips are even. Peel off a small bundle of fibers and measure them against the hook shank so they are a shank length long.

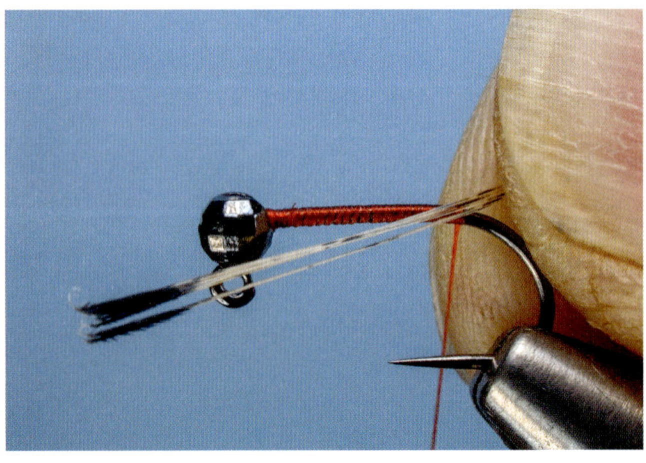

4. Lay the CDL fibers in at an angle on the bend of the hook to capture them with the thread.

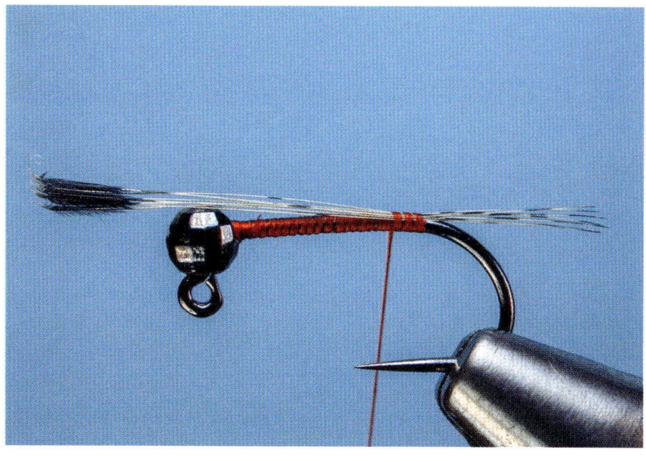

5. Let the first turn of thread over the tails roll the fibers to the top of the hook shank. Make a narrow band of thread at the bend to anchor them in place.

6. Spiral-wrap forward over the butt ends of the tailing fibers to just behind the bead. Clip the remaining butt ends flush.

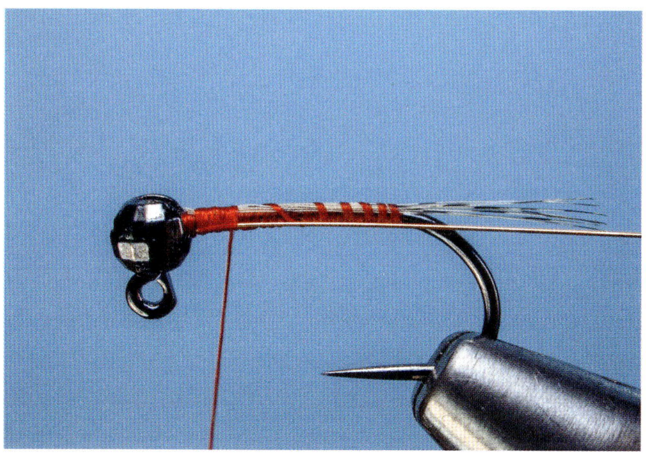

7. Lay the end of a piece of copper wire against the side of the shank and capture it with a narrow band of three or four thread wraps. Pull the front end of the wire down even with the front end of the thread wrap and align the wire to the near side of the hook shank.

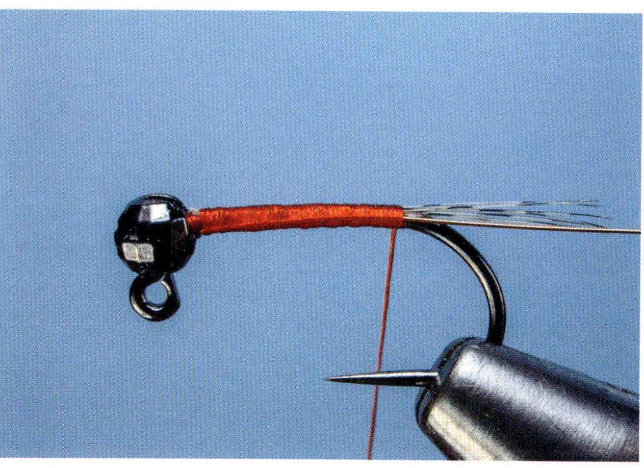

8. Wrap back over the wire—taking care to keep it along the near side of the hook—all the way back to the base of the tail. Make a single, smooth layer of thread over the wire to start the underbody process.

9. Select eight or ten turkey tail fibers from the quill by separating them from the rest. You want to make sure these fibers have some length to them as well as some nice mottling. Clip the turkey section from the quill and then trim the tip end square just a bit back from the tapered tips. Catch the tip end of the feather with a few thread wraps behind the bead with the inside of the feather facing up. Pull the tips down flush to the thread wraps.

10. Wrap back over the turkey quill to the bend of the hook, trying to keep it flat and aligned as you go. Return the thread to just behind the bead with a smooth, even layer of thread.

11. Build a smooth, tapered underbody with the thread to just short of the bead. Don't overbuild this underbody—we want the finished fly to be relatively slim and we still have to wrap the turkey fibers forward over this underbody. Try to make the underbody as smoothly tapered as you can, because lumps and bumps and gaps here will show through on the finished fly. It will still catch fish, but all your friends will make fun of you.

12. Add a drop of head cement to the thread underbody in preparation for the next step. This little shot of cement will help bind the fibers in place and make the fly a bit more durable.

13. Begin wrapping the turkey fibers forward as you might on a Pheasant Tail. Keep the fibers lying flat across the hook as you wrap and don't let them twist.

14. Wrap the turkey right up to the back of the bead; you can go ahead and jam it right up against the bead. This bulk will help to finish the body shape and act as an underbody for the thorax. Clip the excess turkey flush behind the bead and make a couple wraps over the stubs.

15. Spiral-wrap the wire forward from the bend over the turkey to the back of the bead. Tie the wire off with a few tight turns and helicopter the end to break it off.

16. Peel a *very* small amount of hot pink Ice Dub from the package. We are going to twist this dubbing on tightly and we don't want too much. Twist the dubbing onto the thread into the tightest rope you can manage. Pinch your fingers together tightly and make long rolling motions with your fingers to really cinch the dubbing down. Apply the dubbing to only an inch or two of thread; the more thread you use, the more bulk you'll have.

17. Dub a small collar behind the bead, ending with the bare thread hanging at the back edge of the bead. The thorax should be just a skosh bigger than the abdomen, as seen here—exactly one skosh.

18. Build up a narrow band of thread between the front edge of the dubbing collar and the back edge of the bead. This band of red thread is part of the fly and should be prominent, but not oversized. Whip-finish over the band of thread and clip the working thread. Add a shot of head cement to the thread head.

16

COPPER JOHN

A proliferation of parts and pieces from a variety of patterns, the Copper John highlights several worthwhile techniques. Biot tails, a tapered and weighted underbody, wire abdomen, two layer wingcases, and epoxy or light-cured acrylic work all come into play on this fly.

Not just a great fly to fish, the Copper John is a fantastic pattern from a pedagogical standpoint as well. Mastering this somewhat complicated fly is something that nearly every tier I know has struggled with. While not a terribly difficult pattern to tie, the Copper John does have a lot of parts and uses several different techniques in its construction. Any pattern with half as many pieces or just one or two specialized techniques would be considered no big thing by most tiers, but add all these components together and even the best tiers run into a few hitches. There's not much else you could put on a fly that isn't already on the Copper John, but each piece has a purpose.

Let's start with those biot tails. I once asked JB why *biot* tails when this fly, to me anyway, seems like more of a mayfly-profile nymph. Biot tails have always suggested a stonefly nymph pattern in my mind, and now when I think about it, I am not exactly sure why that is . . . probably from tying too many Prince Nymphs over the years. John agreed that the Copper does indeed match mayfly nymphs quite well, but he settled on the split biot tail because of the durability it provides over those conventional hackle-fiber tails. Seems John

John Barr (left) is not only a fly design savant, but he is also a superb fisherman. All great flies are the result of on-the-water testing.

didn't mind so much if the fly didn't match *perfectly* as long as it held up well. He's a no-nonsense kind of guy, so this thought process was something I could get behind.

Next comes the wire body; it's a stroke of genius, compounded by the advent of a plethora of wire colors to play with. The wire body is durable, so much so that I can honestly say I've never seen a Copper John with an abdomen that had come apart. That wire body is also heavy. Its color is easily adaptable thanks to the wide range of shades available, and it's malleable to the point of taking nearly any shape you can imagine. That wire body turned out to be a really, really good idea! Red, copper, and copper-brown colors have become my favorites on this fly but there really is no limit to the variations.

Then we have that pesky wing case. A strip of Thin Skin is topped with a strand of pearl Flashabou for sparkle, then top-coated with a layer of five-minute epoxy. Tiers often ask: Why not skip the Thin Skin and just use a wider strip of flash for the wing case? We do this not only because the Thin Skin keeps the epoxy coat from bleeding down into the peacock herl thorax and legs, but it also stays on top of the fly to create a nicely bulged wing case profile. This added epoxy coat also magnifies the flash aspect of the fly and lends a three-dimensional effect to the pattern as well as increasing durability. Talk about a design element!

I have more recently become fond of using a new one-part UV-set polymer called Clear Cure Goo in place of epoxy on nearly all my flies that require an epoxy top coat. As it is but a single step, as opposed to two-part epoxy, CCG is much less messy, produces absolutely no waste, and can be instantly cured in place with the requisite UV lamp. While two-part epoxy certainly gets the job done, CCG has my endorsement as a viable substitute that will make this intimidating portion of this fly a lot more appealing to the tier.

John reasoned that peacock herl just had to be the thorax on this fly due to its inherent fish-catching powers, a decision I absolutely agree with. The normally fragile peacock herl is, on this pattern, rendered much more durable than normal because it is covered by that epoxy-coated wing case and anchored well inside the pattern itself. Finally, hen saddle fiber legs were chosen, again as a more durable alternative to the original Hungarian partridge feather legs that John started with. While partridge is indeed a prettier feather, the hen saddle fibers are tougher and available in a wider range of mottled shades and colors. It doesn't hurt anyone's feeling that they are much less expensive as well.

When you break down the parts of this fly and consider the rigorous criteria that John employed in its design, it really becomes an amazing creation. All the parts were deliberately chosen to imitate a variety of creepy-crawlies and be durable over the long haul. People laugh when I say that I have had the same size 10 red Copper John in my fly box for well over ten years now. I tied it in that extra-big size for use as a heavier weighted fly in a hopper-copper-dropper rig for some of the faster-moving runs on the Colorado River. I've fished this same single fly over and over for years now, and through some strange stroke of luck have not only never lost it, but it's still holding together perfectly. Of course I've cursed myself to dropping it in the river the next time I am out merely by mentioning this now, but my point is that a properly tied Copper John is an incredibly durable pattern that really only fears rocks and snags on the river bottom. The fly never seems to fall apart and catches fish like nobody's business.

COPPER JOHN (RED)

Hook: #10-18 TMC 5262
Bead: Gold tungsten, sized to hook
Weight: Lead wire, sized to hook
Thread: Black 70-denier UTC or 8/0 Uni
Tail: Brown goose biots
Abdomen: Red Ultra Wire, sized to hook
Flash: Pearl Flashabou
Wing case: Black Thin Skin
Thorax: Peacock herl
Legs: Mottled brown hen saddle
Coating: 30-minute epoxy (according to John Barr himself), but if you wanted to use Clear Cure Goo here, I won't tell. I use the goo.

TUNGSTEN RUBBER-LEG COPPER JOHN

Hook: #12-18 TMC 2499SP-BL
Thread: Black 8/0 Uni
Bead: Black tungsten
Weight: .015" lead wire
Tail: Black goose biots
Abdomen: One strand black Brassie UTC wire and one strand silver small UTC wire
Flash: Single strand silver holographic Flashabou
Wing case: Black Thin Skin, coated with epoxy
Legs: Round black rubber legs (small)
Thorax: Bronze peacock Arizona Synthetic Dubbing

HOOK TO WIRE SIZE

#12	Medium
#14-16	Brassie
#18-20	Small

BEAD TO HOOK SIZE

1/4"	#2-4
7/32"	#2-8
3/16"	#4-8
5/32"	#8-12
1/8"	#10-14
7/64"	#14-16
3/32"	#14-18
5/64"	#18-22
1/16"	#22-26

LEAD WIRE TO HOOK SIZE

.035"	#4 and bigger
.030"	#4-6
.025"	#6-10
.020"	#12-14
.015"	#14-16
.010"	#18 and smaller

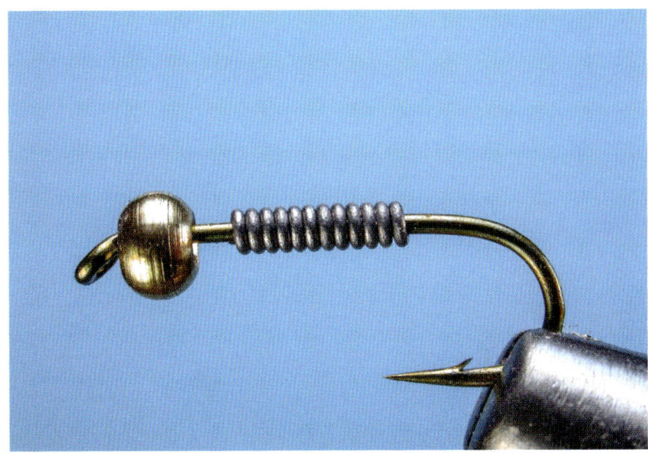

1. Place the bead on the hook by putting the point of the hook into the smaller hole on the front of the bead. Slide the bead up to the hook eye. Wrap thirteen turns of the appropriately sized lead wire (see chart) onto the hook shank. Make these wraps from the back of the hook to the front. Break the ends off the lead on either end of the wraps by pushing on the lead with your thumbnail.

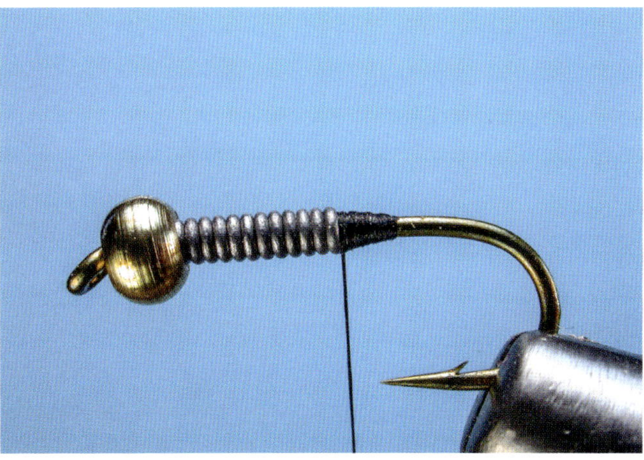

2. Shove the lead wraps up into the back of the bead, countersinking the wraps into the recess.Start the tying thread at the back edge of the lead wraps. Build a smooth taper from the bare hook shank up to the diameter of the lead wire. This little thread dam will prevent the lead wraps from separating as we overwrap them later. Continue wrapping a smooth thread base back to the bend of the hook, and then forward again all the way up to the back of the lead. Wrap the thread all the way back to the bend once more, maintaining the taper as you go.

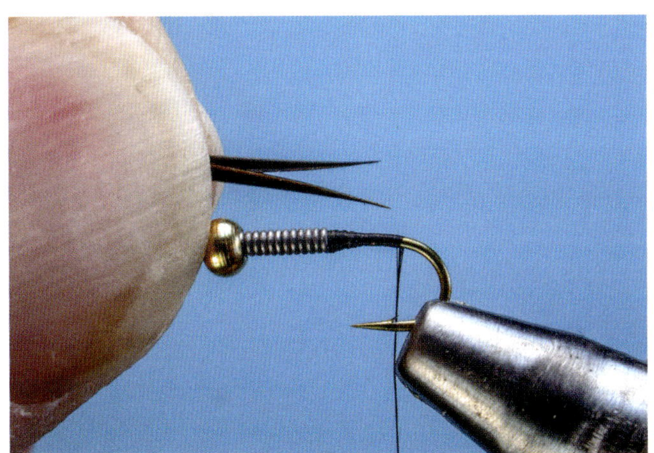

3. Select two matched biots from the quill. I like to pull two that are right next to each other to assure that they are the same width and length. Oppose the curves of the biots by placing them back-to-back so they curve away from each other and even their tips. Measure the biots against the hook shank so they are equal to half a shank's length.

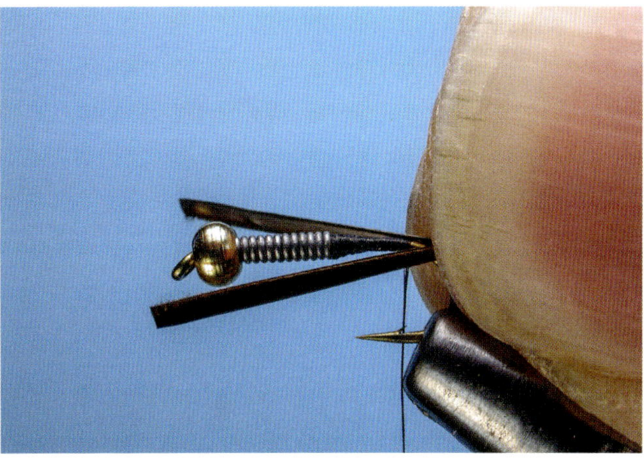

4. Place the opposed biots at the bend of the hook with one on each side of the hook shank.

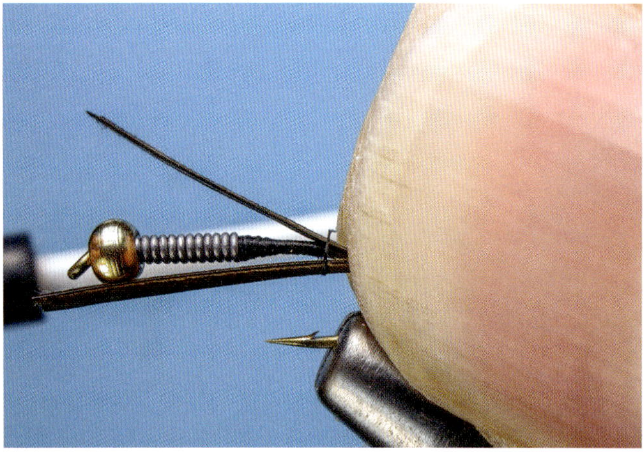

5. Turn the biots so they are slightly off-center toward the near side of the hook. Place a single turn of thread over the biots. This turn will only hold the biots in place, slightly to the near side of the hook.

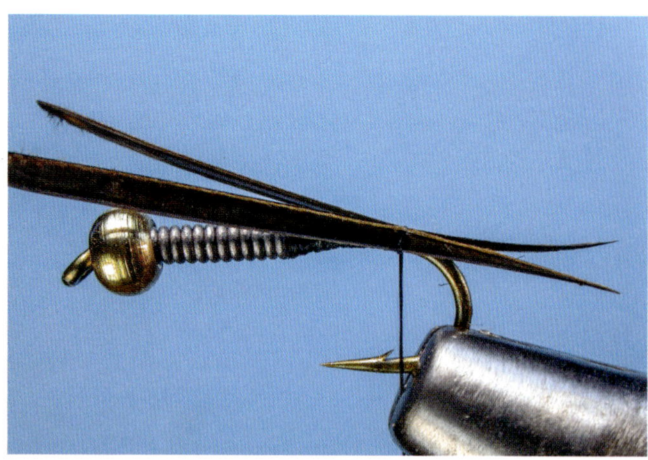

6. The biots should be on either side of the hook shank—*not centered* on the shank, but twisted slightly toward the near side of the hook.

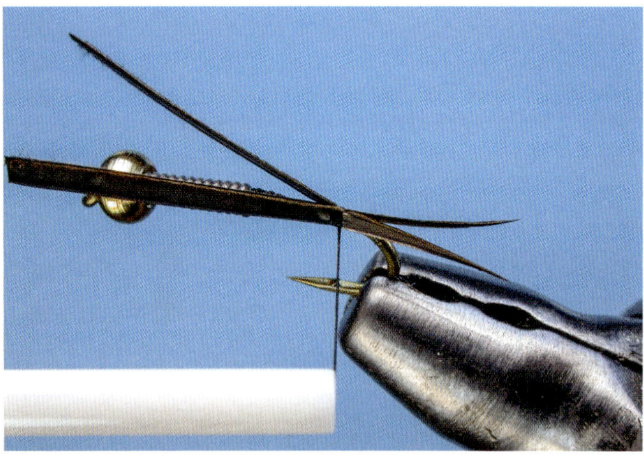

7. Pull the tying thread toward you to tighten the loop of thread over the first loose wrap, which will pull the biots to top dead center on the hook shank and leave you with a perfectly centered tail.

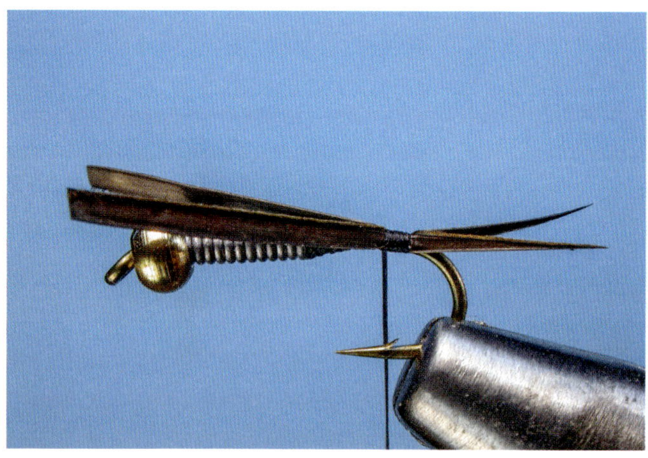

8. Wrap forward over the butt ends, forming a short band of thread. This band will hold the tails securely in place.

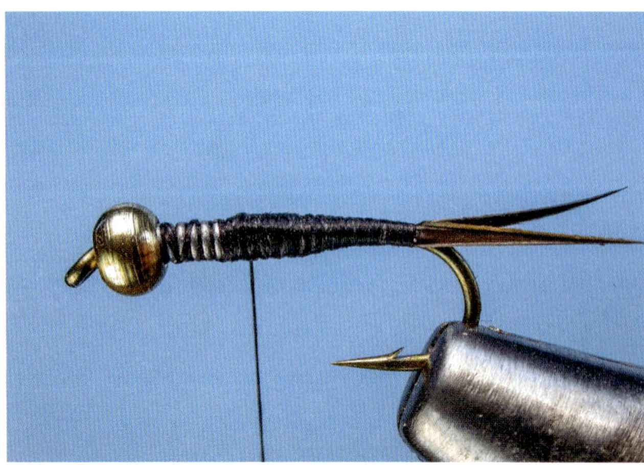

9. Clip the butt ends of the biots and continue wrapping the thread up to the back of the bead. Return the thread to the two-thirds point on the shank, making sure to keep a smoothly tapered underbody.

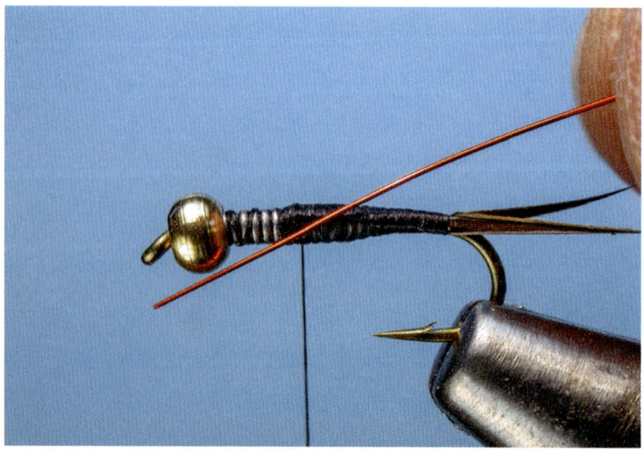

10. Cut a length of copper wire about six or eight inches long and tie it in at the front of the thread underbody, using the right-angle technique, along the near side of the hook shank. Pull the front end of the wire down flush to the thread wraps.

11. Wrap back over the wire to the bend of the hook, forming a smooth and even underbody. We need this underbody to be as smooth as possible because the overbody will mirror any lumps or bumps we have here.

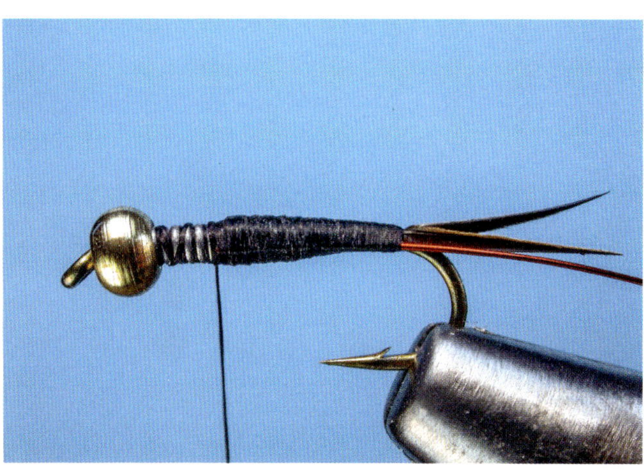

12. Return the thread to the front of the underbody. As you begin to wrap forward from the bend, be sure to make the thread wraps concentric and as tight as possible near the tail. We want to make sure the wire is completely and securely anchored at the bend of the hook.

13. Bring the wire up and over the top of the hook for the start of the first wrap of wire. This turn should be butted right at the front edge of the tails.

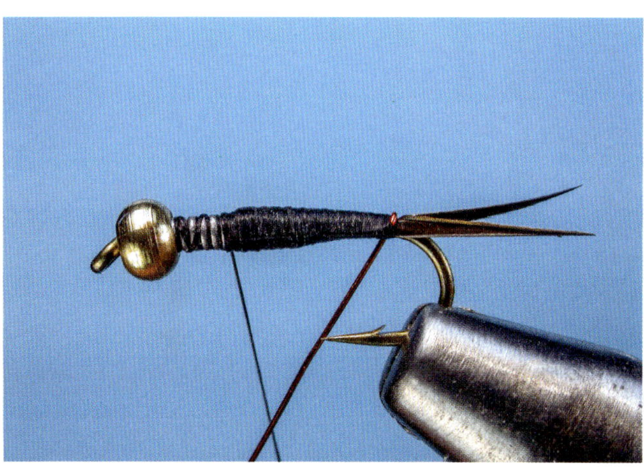

14. Bring the wire down under the hook and then reach forward with it around the point of the hook. The next step will make a big difference in how tightly butted you make the body wraps, so pay attention.

15. Bring the wire back in line with the front edge of the first wrap. You have to bring the wire forward around the point of the hook, but more importantly, you must bring it back again to line it up with the previous wrap. If you don't bring it back in line you'll have a gap in the wraps on the bottom and a wonky angle to follow the rest of the way up the shank. You'll need to do this same thing for the next three or four turns until you clear the hook point.

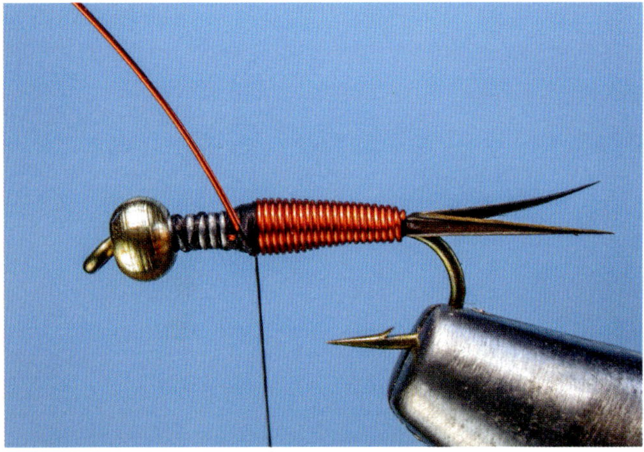

16. Continue wrapping the wire forward with one turn directly in front of the last. Tilt the wire back a bit as you bring it over the top of the hook; you will use the previous wrap of wire as a guide for the next wrap.

Wrap the wire forward all the way up to and just slightly past the end of the thread underbody. Bring the end of the wire up above the hook and tie it off with a few firm wraps of thread. Don't worry when the wire wraps spread out a bit here on the front edge. The descending taper will cause the wire to spread a bit but this will eventually be covered by our thorax and wing case, so don't get worked up.

17. Helicopter the end of the wire to break it off flush. Cut a length of pearl Flashabou and tie it in on top of the shank behind the bead and wrap back over it to the 60 percent point. I hold the flash in place with my material-hand thumb, slightly to the near side of the shank as I bring a wrap of thread up and over it. The thread torque will twist the flash to the top of the shank and center it there.

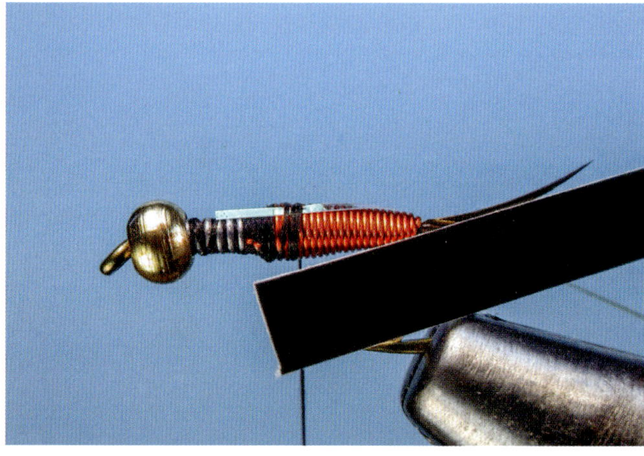

18. Cut a strip of black Thin Skin from the sheet; it should be just slightly narrower than the gap of the hook. Leave the paper backing attached while you cut the strip. If you get all fancy and try to remove the backing from the whole sheet, the Thin Skin will curl up into an unusable mess.

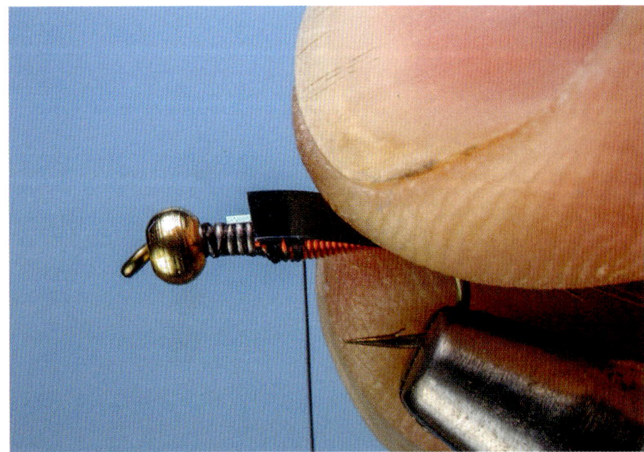

19. Press the Thin Skin flat in place with your thumb at the 60 percent point. Capture the Thin Skin with a few tight turns of thread at the 60 percent point.

20. Wrap forward over the front end of the Thin Skin wing case, binding it down to the shank up to the back edge of the bead.

21. Select a half-dozen peacock herls and clip their tips so they are square. Tie the herls in by their tips at the base of the wing case with a couple taut wraps of thread.

22. Pull the butt ends of the peacock to draw the tips down behind the bead. Wrap back tightly over the tips of the peacock herl up to the base of the wing case, then return the thread to the back of the bead.

23. Wrap the peacock herl forward all the way up to the bead. Make sure the last wrap of herl is snug against the bead, and then tie off the herl with a couple firm wraps of thread. Clip the excess herl flush against the shank.

24. Select a large hen saddle feather and break the fluff off the end to leave only the pretty, mottled fibers. Preen a gap-width clump of fibers out away from the stem so their tips are even and then peel them from the center stem. While taking care to keep the tips even, measure these fibers against the shank so they extend from the back edge of the bead to the point on the hook.

25. Reach in and pinch the hen fibers against the near side of the shank with your material hand. Make a couple turns of thread over the base of the hen fibers right at the back edge of the bead. These thread wraps should cinch tightly down between the bead and the absolute front edge of the peacock herl.

26. Check the length of the hen fibers to ensure that they reach to the hook point and are sitting squarely on the near side of the hook shank.

27. Repeat the above process on the far side of the hook. Even out a clump of hen fibers, peel them from the stem, and measure them so they are equal in length to the clump on the near side of the hook.

28. Pinch this second clump of fibers in place along the far side of the hook just like you did with the first bunch. Make a couple turns over the second clump of hen fibers on the far side of the hook before you let go of the tips.

29. Double-check to be sure both leg bunches are the same length. If one side is longer than the other, you can gently pull on the butt ends to shorten them slightly.

30. Reach in with the tips of your fine scissors and clip the butts as close to the bead as you can. Repeat this step on both sides.

31. With your thread hand, pull the Thin Skin wing case over the thorax, making sure it is centered. As you stretch it slightly, take a few tight turns over it right behind the bead using your material hand.

32. Pull the flash over the top of the wing case, again making certain that it is centered on the wing case, and tie it down behind the bead as well.

33. Clip both the Thin Skin and the flash as closely as you can. Build a smooth thread head to cover the stubs.

34. Whip-finish and clip the thread behind the bead.

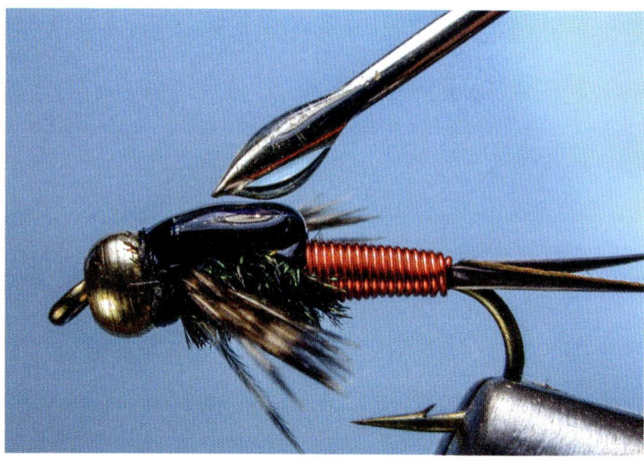

35. With the fly in the vise, reach in and sweep the legs down while you apply a drop of Clear Cure Goo to the wing case. I try to work the goo onto the back edge of the bead and the front edge of the wire body to anchor it in place securely. Cook the Goo with UV light.

36. Finished fly. Make sure the wire abdomen doesn't show any spaces and the thorax blends smoothly into the front end. Always take a close look at your finished product and make note of any errors or flubs along the way in order to be more aware of them on the next one. Each fly you tie is experience for the next one!

17

SPARKLE PUPA

Some flies just never lose their luster, and Gary LaFontaine's Sparkle Pupa is at the top of that list. With a timelessly innovative take on the shuck and collar, this fly will always produce fish and allows you to expand your repertoire of skills.

This pattern goes back a long way. While there are hundreds of newer, flashier caddis pupa patterns out there now, the good old Sparkle Pupa remains pretty tough to beat. Developed by the late Gary LaFontaine, this simple fly features a shuck over the abdomen that creates a halo of light around the fly. LaFontaine reasoned that this airy shuck represented the gas bubbles surrounding the real deal as it emerged toward the surface. I would guess that he was more than a little right. There are not a lot of patterns that have had the longevity of this fly, and I and other anglers worldwide have continued to hammer fish with it for a long time now.

While I am sure there are several appropriate materials to use for this wonderful shuck, I have used Sparkle Yarn on this pattern for many years. Sparkle Yarn, aka Aunt Lydia's Sparkle Yarn, is a rug-yarn fiber with a bit of sheen to it. Possessing just the right amount of sparkle and stiffness, Sparkle Yarn works perfectly for this fly. It comes in a three-ply strand that is easily separated, and I find that sparser is better when tying this shuck. Keep in mind that the shuck is an outside element you're trying to represent, rather than an

The Sparkle Pupa is an old fly that has not lost its effectiveness, though most commercial versions are tied incorrectly. Sparseness is the key to tying a good one.

actual part of the real bug—an ephemeral, sparse, ghostlike apparition is what you are after rather than a big, thick glob piled around the body. Every single commercially tied version of this fly that I have ever seen is tied too heavily, in my opinion, so keep that in mind before you run out and buy one as a sample to guide your work.

A single ply of the three strands is more than enough to create the perfect silhouette of the shuck around the abdomen. I like to brush it out a bit to help separate the fibers, and I take pains to evenly distribute them around the shank for more even coverage. Gary didn't rib his original pattern; this feature is something I have added to my version simply because the natural is so prominently ribbed and it's so easy to do. As for the thorax/head, I love the look that a folded marabou collar gives a fly and have always used this on my patterns. The marabou flows back over the front of the body and pulses and moves in the slightest current. It doesn't hurt that it looks exactly like the snotty, gooey mess that caddis pupae are, either. This technique can be a little tricky to get the hang of and requires marabou with long flues radiating off the barbs themselves. Often sold as Woolly Bugger marabou, these shorter feathers are softer, have wider flues, and are silkier than the usual marabou. Pay close attention to the tutorial regarding the head of the fly, and I will walk you through the proper method of creating this great effect.

I have fished this fly a ton over the years and it was one of my favorite afternoon patterns on the South Platte back in the day. While there are good numbers of caddis on the Platte, the Sparkle Pupa worked well even when there was no sign of hatching caddis. I often employed it as a more subtle searching pattern than a true hatch-matcher. It seems the fish were pretty used to encountering caddis pupae and would eat the fly with good regularity. Of course, if you add in an actual caddis hatch this fly really comes into its own. Fished down along the bottom before the hatch or dangling behind a dry during it, the Sparkle Pupa gets pounded. The emergent version shown here with a sparse deer hair wing can even be greased and fished dry right in the film as a sort of crippled caddis emerger, often with incredible results.

I tie mine in a pale olive tone, as well as in brighter green and cream-colored versions, usually using Hareline Dubbin's Hare-Tron which is a mix of rabbit fur and Antron that adds a nice bit of shine and sparkle to the abdomen. I typically tie them in sizes 16 and 18; you can of course tailor the colors and sizes to meet your own needs. I show the fully dressed emergent Sparkle Pupa here in the tutorial but admit that I fish the deep-sparkle version (sans wing) more often. I figured it was easy enough to tell you to leave the wing out if so desired.

SPARKLE PUPA

Hook: #14-20 TMC 100 SPBL
Thread: Camel 8/0 Uni
Shuck: Tan Sparkle Yarn
Abdomen: Pale olive Hare-Tron
Rib: Tying thread
Wing: Natural fine-tipped deer hair
Head: Black marabou

DEEP SPARKLE PUPA

Hook: #14-20 TMC 100 SPBL
Thread: Camel 8/0 Uni
Shuck: Tan Sparkle Yarn
Abdomen: Pale olive Hare-Tron
Rib: Tying thread
Head: Black marabou

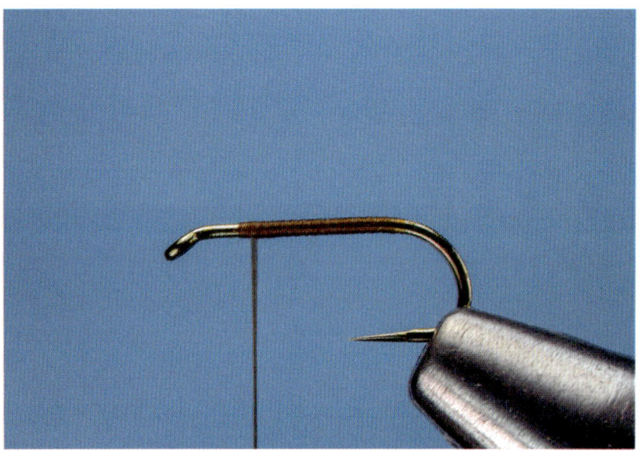

1. Start the thread about two eye lengths back from the eye and wrap a thread base back to the bend and forward again to the starting point.

2. Cut a short length of Sparkle Yarn from the card and separate the three strands.

3. Select a single strand and brush it out to separate the fibers. I lay the strand on my desktop and run a dubbing brush from the center out toward the ends to remove the twist and spread it out. On a size 14, you may need the entire strand, perhaps even a bit more, but on an 18 you'll want to thin the strand down just a little bit. This overbody and shuck should be sparse and only serve to create the illusion of air bubbles and sparkle over the abdomen, so keep that in mind.

4. Tie the square-cut end of the Sparkle Yarn on at the starting point on top of the shank with a tight band of thread.

5. Pull the long end of the Sparkle Yarn down so it splits evenly on either side of the hook shank.

6. Spiral-wrap the thread over the yarn to the bend of the hook and anchor it in place with a couple stacked turns at the back.

7. Dub a somewhat loose strand of dubbing onto the thread and burn up the bare thread between the end of the dubbing and the hook shank by making wraps near the tie-in. We want to wrap this dubbing from the front to the back, so once the dubbing closely approaches the hook shank, be sure to be at the tie-in area.

8. Wrap the dubbing from the tie-in point back to the bend of the hook, building a reverse taper as you go. Caddis pupae are fatter at the rear end than the front, so we want to mimic that here. End with bare thread hanging at the hook bend; the bare tying thread is about to become our ribbing. I'm crafty like that.

9. Spiral-wrap the tying thread forward over the dubbing to the tie-in point, creating body segments along the dubbing.

10. Make a thread base from the front of the abdomen to the hook eye and back again. Spread the Sparkle Yarn out a bit at the bend with your fingers. You don't want it clumped up, just evenly spread out.

11. Press the tip of your material-hand index finger up against the bend of the hook, pushing the yarn forward and splaying it out at the bend.

12. Reach in with your thread hand and grab the loose ends of the yarn, taking care to keep them spread around the hook and encompassing the abdomen.

13. Pull the ends of the Sparkle Yarn tight and out past the hook eye. Again, make sure the yarn is evenly distributed around the hook shank in this step.

14. Without letting go of the ends of the yarn, push your pinched fingertips back, buckling the yarn slightly over the abdomen and introducing some slack.

15. Hold the yarn in place and make a loose wrap or two to anchor the yarn down. You don't want the thread wraps to move the yarn from its evenly distributed state.

16. You ought to have an overbody that looks something like this. Note that the husk is sparse and translucent.

17. Use the tips of your scissors to lift a few strands of yarn from the top of the body. I try to pull the slack out of the strands as well as slide a bit of extra length from the excess ends out front under the thread wraps. This produces an ever-so-slightly longer shuck.

18. Clip the lifted yarn strands flush against the front of the body. The fibers will fall back off the bend of the hook and magically form a trailing shuck and sparkle trail. LaFontaine was pretty crafty too.

19. Clip the excess Sparkle Yarn from the front of the shank and wrap down over the stubs. Leave the thread hanging at the front edge of the abdomen.

20. Cut, clean, and stack a small clump of fine deer hair. Measure the hair against the hook so it extends from the front of the abdomen to the bend of the hook.

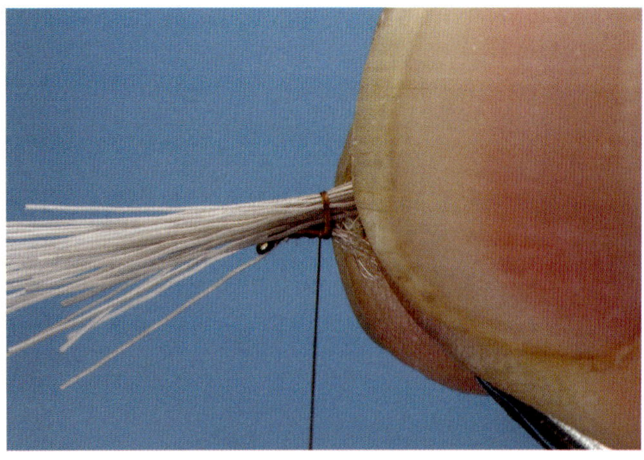

21. Grab the tips of the hair along with the hook shank and hold them tightly at their measured length. Make two taut—but not tight—turns of thread over the hair at the front of the body.

22. Pull the thread toward you to flare the butt ends while still holding tightly onto the tips of the hair.

23. Work the thread forward with four or five more wraps through the butt ends of the hair, further anchoring them down, but stop well short of the hook eye with the thread. Gather the butt ends of the hair above the hook and clip them off flush to the hook.

24. The leftover butt ends should be trimmed flush to the hook.

25. Select a wide marabou feather that has bushy barbs. That skinny, ratty stuff won't cut it here; you want the type of marabou typically sold as Woolly Bugger marabou, as it has long flues and thin stems. Note that I am not talking about the actual center quill of the feather, but rather the individual fibers protruding from the barbules.

Peel off about a dozen marabou strands from the center stem. This photo better illustrates the long flues we are looking for. Think of each marabou fiber as a tiny hackle feather and look at the barb length—you want it about as wide as the gap of the hook.

26. Bunch the marabou strands together and wet the tips with a bit of saliva. I just lick my fingertips and run them down the tip of the feather, but you can go ahead and stick it in your mouth if you're into that sort of thing. The point being, you want to separate these fibers as you would a soft-hackle feather, like a partridge feather being tied in by the tip. The spit helps keep the tip fibers pointing forward and the rest of the fibers sticking out from the stem. Tie the entire bunch of marabou in at the division point at the base of the wing. Try not to trap any fibers behind the tie-in point, but do what you will with the fibers sticking forward on the tips of the feather strands.

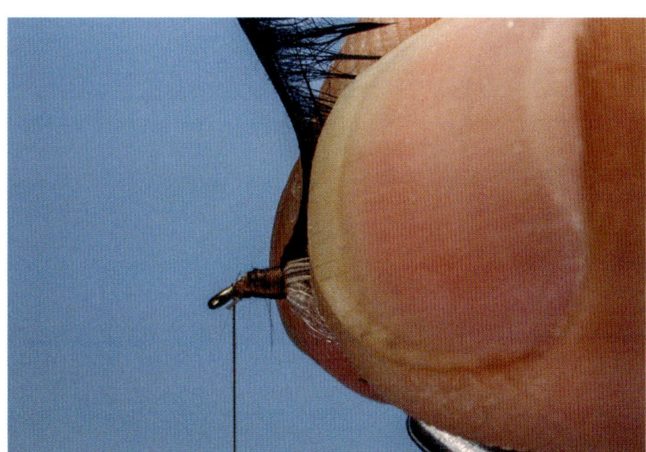

27. Clip the excess tips flush and then wet your fingertips again. We are now going to fold the marabou flues to one side, exactly as we did with the partridge feather on the Soft-Hackle. These fibers fold a fair bit more easily than the partridge, as the marabou fibers are much softer. You're really just sort of preening these fibers back like you were folding them, but their inherent softness will prevent them from actually creasing as a stiffer fiber would. That little bit of moisture on your fingertips is going to be what holds these fibers temporarily in place here. Don't get all slobbery about it; just make sure you have enough spit in there to get the job done. Make sure the thread is hanging at the hook eye.

28. Once you have folded the marabou, hold the strands in the tips of your fingers. I can prevent them from twisting more easily with my hands than with a pair of hackle pliers. Begin to wrap the marabou strands forward, treating them exactly as you did the soft-hackle feather. Make a turn, preen the flues back, and then make another turn in front. You want to make two or three turns but no more, even though it's tempting. Too many turns will overlap the fibers and kill the flowing effect we are after.

29. Once you reach the hook eye, tie the marabou fibers off with a couple tight wraps of thread.

30. Clip the excess marabou flush and build a small thread head over the butt ends. Whip-finish and clip the thread.

31. Tweak the hook eye to one side with your fingertip a bit in order to "spring" the hook and make the marabou fibers pop more upright . . . that is, if you didn't slobber all over them, in which case you just have to wait for them to dry a bit and remember next time that it's a fly and not your prom date.

32. Come in with the tips of your scissors and trim the marabou fibers flush along the top of the fly, leaving the flowing stuff only on the sides and bottom of the fly.

33. The finished Sparkle Pupa. Note how you can clearly see the body through the overbody husk; the body is obviously separate from that husk, not a big fat ball of Sparkle Yarn that has God knows what hidden under it.

34. You can omit the deer-hair wing and get what's known as a Deep Sparkle Pupa. I have fished both of these patterns all through the water column and find them equally effective. The deer-hair wing does make that version slightly more buoyant however, should the need arise to grease the fly and fish it dry.

TWENTY-INCHER

Perhaps one of the most popular stonefly nymph patterns ever, the Twenty-Incher is great fly tying exercise as well. Using everyday materials to create a tapered abdomen and robust thorax, this pattern illustrates that you don't always need a boxful of new materials to create a fresh pattern.

I know I'm finally (or really) getting old when I think back about how many flies I can remember from their origination. The Twenty-Incher is one of those painfully sharp reminders of my age. I recall first coming in contact with this fly way back when I was a kid. In Colorado's Roaring Fork Valley, a somewhat secret pattern was being passed around among guides and fly-shop guys and I, being a commercial tier, was let in on the secret. One of the biggest advantages to tying for independent fly shops is getting access to the top-secret developments of some of the best guides on the planet. The Twenty-Incher was quietly shown to me along with an order for twenty dozen of them, and that was really something for a kid my age.

Just the name of this fly elicits memories of a mythical pattern that I had heard an awful lot about long before I ever had the chance to actually see the dang thing. I recall thinking, "Anything called a Twenty-Incher has got to be good!" Of course, part of that was my youthful imagination running off with dreams of giant Roaring Fork rainbows and browns, but in the years since this pattern has become the staple large stonefly pattern in not just my fly box, but in those of a good many excellent guides and anglers as well.

This pattern still throws a few curves after all these years, and the tying process can be somewhat of a mystery to the casual observer. It features a split biot tail, juicy peacock abdomen (originally ribbed with waxed kite string and now with more easily obtained rayon floss), a thorax of hare's mask dubbing topped with partridge legs, and a turkey quill wing case. Later, a bead head was added to keep the fly down along the bottom, but this pattern has remained virtually unchanged since way back when I was a kid. (You should read the last part of that sentence in a curmudgeonly voice, like I did when I typed it.)

While some of the parts and their tying processes are pretty apparent, I have found over the years that it's easy to mess this fly up. Primarily, I find that the addition of a dubbed underbody—meant to shape and bulk up the abdomen—and the crafty way in which the partridge fiber legs are applied to be sticking points that can make or break this fly. I tie most of my own Twenty-Inchers a bit on the skinny side. While it is really easy to bulk this fly up and turn it into a real meat-and-potatoes kind of pattern, I have found that a slightly skinnier version more accurately replicates the elongated body of a real stonefly nymph. The mixed colors and peacock abdomen of this pattern make it a nice go-between for both dark- and light-colored stones, and the fly can be used effectively to match both shades.

I fish this pattern mostly in the spring, and typically tight to the banks. I generally weight it pretty heavily to keep it down on the bottom in swollen currents, but I still carry a few non–bead head versions with less weight for plying particularly shallow water. One of the biggest advantages to tying your own flies is the ability to tailor the weight of a pattern and create versions of the same fly in various weights. Having a few lightly weighted or unweighted patterns in your box can really come in handy when you find a bunch of early-season fished stacked up on the edge of a riffle feasting on stones. The heavily weighted patterns hang up on the bottom in this shallow water and force you to either lose a bunch of flies or wade out through the fish to retrieve them. A few lighter versions stashed in your box for moments like this are priceless and exactly why you sit at the vise in the evenings.

While not used on the original pattern, adding a coat of epoxy or UV resin to the wing case of the Twenty Incher adds durability and a modern flair. If you opt to add the coating, simply build a thread head behind the bead and skip the dubbed collar.

TWENTY-INCHER

Hook: #4-14 TMC 200
Bead: Gold tungsten, sized to hook
Weight: Lead or nonlead wire
Thread: Black 3/0 Monocord, 6/0 Uni, or 8/0 Uni
Tails: Brown goose biots
Rib: Beige floss
Underbody: Super Fine, any color
Abdomen: Peacock herl
Wing case: Mottled turkey quill
Legs: Hungarian partridge body feather
Thorax: Natural light hare's mask dubbing

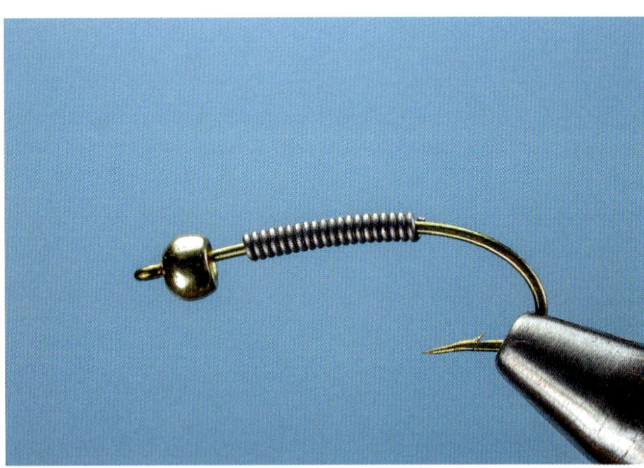

1. Place the bead on the hook and slide it up to the eye. Make ten to twenty wraps of lead wire on the shank and break the ends off with your thumbnail. I'm tying a big fly here so I have weighted this one a bit on the heavy side.

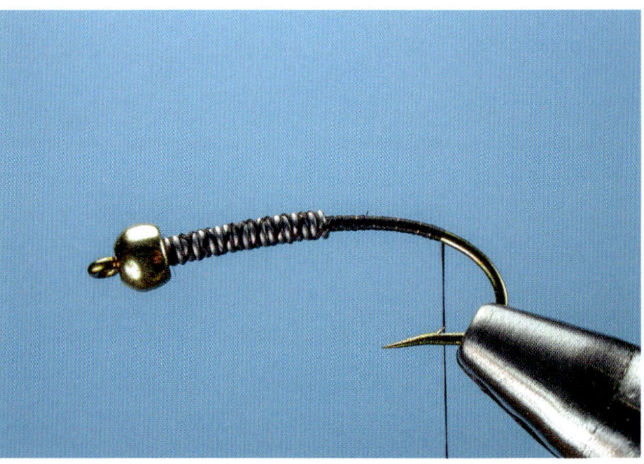

2. Shove the lead wraps up into the back of the bead and then start the thread behind the lead. Wrap forward over the lead, locking it in place, and then return the thread to the bend, building a thread base along the shank as you go. Leave the thread hanging even with the point on the barb.

3. Select two brown goose biots and oppose their curves. Even the tips and hold them by their bases in your thread hand. Measure the biots against the shank so they are about a half shank length long or maybe just a touch longer on a bigger fly.

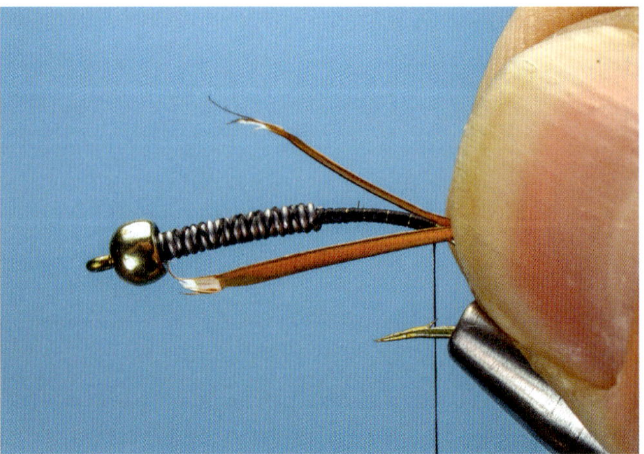

4. Transfer the measured biot tips to your material hand and slide them up from the back of the hook bend, splitting their bases with the hook shank. Tilt the biots just slightly on their axis to the near side of the hook.

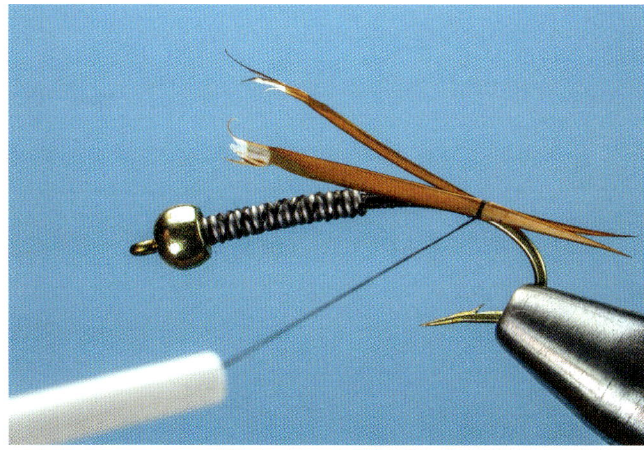

5. Make a single turn over the top of the hook and around the biots while holding them in place. I have removed my hand here to show you what's happening inside my fingertips to prevent you from getting antsy and opening your fingers to look at your own fly's tail. Note that the biots are slightly canted to the near side here; the thread wraps are taut but have not been tightened down yet.

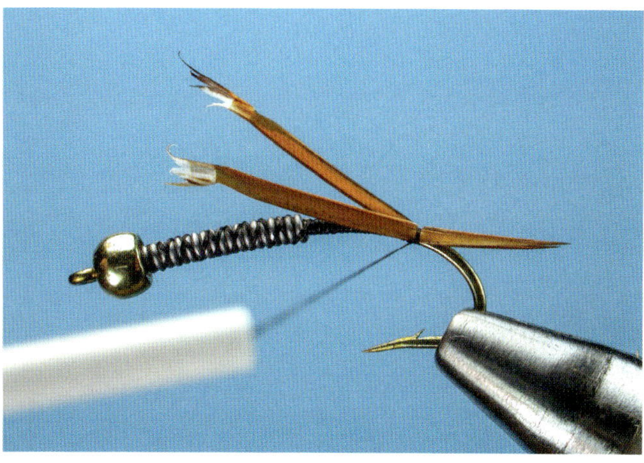

6. Pull the thread toward you to cinch the wrap down and the biots will roll slightly to their correct position of top dead center on the hook shank. If they're not perfectly even, you can tweak the long ends a bit before you make any additional wraps and position them manually if needed.

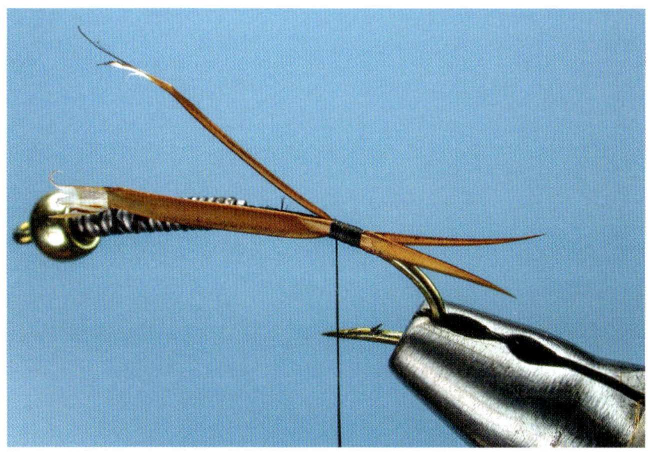

7. Once you're happy with the biot placement, wrap forward over the butt ends to lock them down. Make sure these wraps only go forward of the initial wraps, as anything behind that first turn will affect the tail alignment.

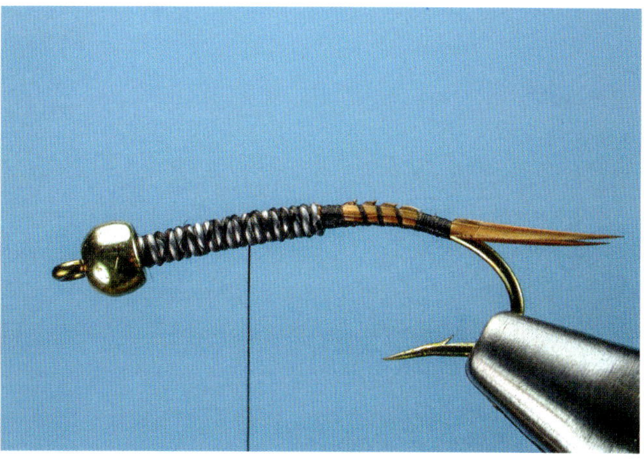

8. Continue spiral-wrapping forward over the butt ends of the biots to the back of the lead wraps, where you will cut the excess biots flush.

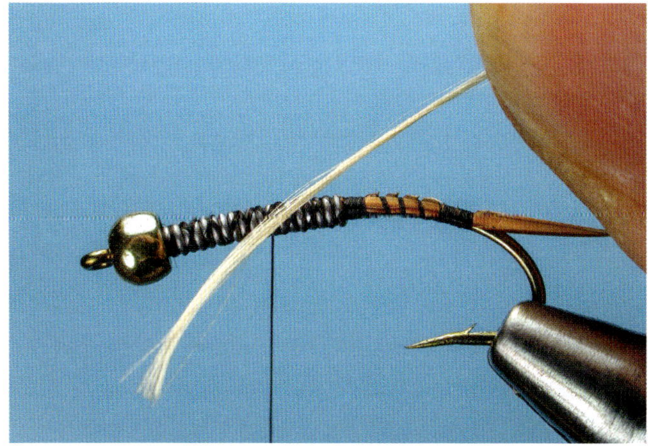

9. Cut a strand of floss from the spool and split it in half as you did for the Soft-Hackle, or in even smaller portions for smaller patterns. Lay the floss along the shank somewhere around the 60 percent point.

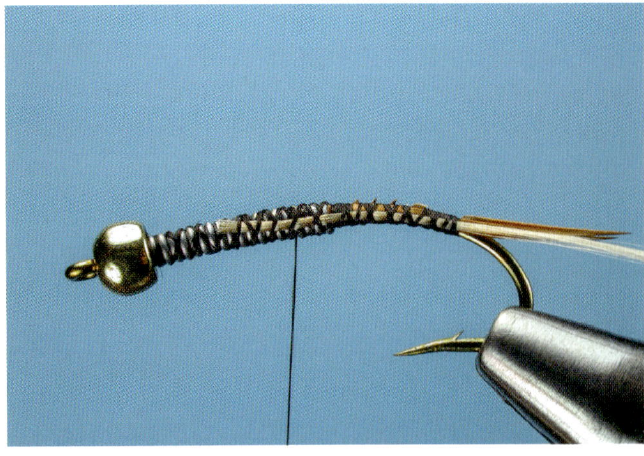

10. Capture the end of the floss with a wrap of thread and pull the front end down flush to the thread wrap. Spiral-wrap back over the floss to the hook bend and then forward to the tie-in point. Let the floss hang out the back of the hook for now.

11. Apply a tight strand of dubbing to the thread and build a tapered underbody from the base of the tails to about a bead length behind the bead. Keep this underbody slightly undersized--it will fill out the peacock overbody and create a more tapered body, but if it's overdone it will make the fly too fat.

12. Spiral-wrap the thread over the underbody back to the hook bend. Select six or eight bushy peacock herls (for a size 6, fewer for smaller patterns) and clip their tips even.

13. Tie the peacock herl in by the tips at the bend of the hook, then spiral-wrap the thread forward to the front of the dubbed underbody.

14. Wrap the peacock herl forward, taking care to keep the herls lying alongside each other rather than twisted up into a bunch. Keeping them flat will allow for the fibers to slope back toward the bend and create a really cool-looking abdomen. Tie the herls off at the front of the underbody and clip the excess.

15. Now spiral-wrap the floss forward through the peacock herl with evenly spaced turns. On a big fly, you have room for more turns, but on a small fly you'll probably want to make fewer turns. Tie the floss off at the front and clip the extra.

16. Clip a section of turkey quill from the stem (either tail or wing will work fine here) that is just a bit narrower than the hook gap. Cut the tip end of the slip square. Wrap the thread back over the front end of the abdomen to the 60 percent point.

17. Lay the turkey slip flat on top of the abdomen with the inside of the feather facing up. Tie it down tightly by its tip with a narrow band of thread at the 60 percent point, then spiral forward over the remaining tips. This slip should be centered on top of the abdomen.

18. Select a nicely mottled Hungarian partridge body feather and strip the fluff from its base. You want a feather that has barbs that are no longer than half a shank length. Hold the tip of the feather in your fingertips and stroke the remaining barbs back toward the base of the feather to create a division point where the fibers change direction. You'll be left with a triangle-shaped feather tip.

19. Turn the feather over so the inside of the curve is facing up, and then tie it in at the base of the wing case by the triangle-shaped tip. Don't tie right up to the point on the triangle; leave a tiny bit exposed to aid in the folding process to come. Wrap forward over the remaining partridge fibers to the bead and trim any excess. You should now have a turkey slip tied in with the inside facing up flat on top of the abdomen, followed by a Hungarian partridge feather tied in by its tip right on top of the turkey.

20. Dub the thread with the hare's mask dubbing and begin to build the thorax, starting at the back edge of the bead and working toward the base of the wing case.

21. Work the dubbing all the way back to the base of the wing case then come forward again to the back of the bead, forming an elongated thorax just slightly thicker than the abdomen.

22. Lift the partridge feather up and fold it forward over the top of the dubbed thorax. Stroke the fibers rearward to their natural position on the stem. As you pull the feather forward, there should be bare stem where the feather lines up with the back of the bead. If there isn't, peel a few fibers from each side of the stem until there is.

Tie the partridge feather down right behind the bead with a couple tight turns of thread. Be conscious of pulling the feather off-center as you tie it down—you want it right on top. Clip the excess stem flush.

23. Lift the turkey slip and fold it over the top of the partridge feather and dubbed thorax. Tie the turkey slip down at the back of the bead as well. Make sure the slip lies flat across the top of the thorax in a wide band. Clip the excess turkey slip flush.

24. Apply a thin strand of dubbing to the thread and cover the tie-off area behind the bead with it. Leave the thread hanging at the immediate back edge of the bead before whip-finishing. If you're careful, you can whip-finish and let the thread wraps slide right off the back of the bead and sink them under this dubbing, hiding the whip-finish. If you're not careful, you can make about a hundred wraps of thread here and really bung things up.

25. Top view of the finished fly.

26. Side view of the finished fly.

SPARKLE MIDGE LARVA

Trout are constantly encountering midge larvae and pupae and oftentimes it just takes a bit of sparkle or flash to make your pattern stand out amongst the crowd. The Sparkle Midge Pupa is craftily tied with an internal rib and flash and a colored Micro Tubing overbody that creates a glow from within.

Midges are probably the most common trout stream bugs out there, and there's no arguing that there is an overabundance of patterns to match them. Ranging from simple thread-and-wire configurations to much more complex patterns with multiple components, the sheer enormity of the possibilities is sometimes hard to comprehend. As an experienced tier and fisherman, I can tell you you'll want to tie all of them to start. Then, as you fish and tie more, you'll whittle your selection down to a few "confidence patterns" that you enjoy tying and are productive for you. That being said, this simple little Sparkle Midge Larva pattern is just another option to put in your fly box, filling the requisite needs of a pattern like this: It's slim, ribbed, accurately colored, and has just a tiny bit of fish-attracting sparkle. From a design standpoint, this fly is simple, quick, and easy to tie, uses common materials, and is put together

Having a box stocked with various midge larva and pupa patterns is a good idea for any angler and is almost a law here in Colorado.

in sort of a slick way. It's a nicely ribbed pattern that is durable and attractive to the fish at the same time.

I find midges to be commonly available to the fish throughout the year and a staple food item. Leaner seasons of early spring, late fall, and winter seem to provide the most prolific midge bite, although in some areas (particularly tailwaters) fish will feed heavily on them all through the summer as well. Having a box stocked with various midge larva and pupa patterns is a good idea for any angler and is almost a law here in Colorado. I have a separate fly box devoted to a plethora of midge patterns, and it includes my own designs like the Sparkle Larva and Jujubee as well as traditional favorites like the Brassie and Black Beauty. It's comforting to have some options on a cold winter day when you want to mix things up a bit, and because they're typically so small, it's always easy to jam just a few more into the fly box. Frankly, I know I could get away with midge patterns in sizes 20 and 22, in browns, olives, blacks, whites, and reds, for nearly all of my fishing, and could probably do it with just a few actual patterns—but I am just not that kind of guy. I have a pile of variations on the theme crowding up my head and fly box at any given time. Tying and fishing is fun, and running out of ammo can put a serious damper on that, so I like to stay well stocked with these simple flies.

The Sparkle Midge Larva I'll show here was designed to match the slim, olive-colored midge larvae so prevalent in many of my local waters. Tied with a super-thin micro tubing body wrapped over a dark-colored thread rib, this pattern is incredibly durable. That's because the fine rib is actually on the inside of the fly rather than the outside. Adding a turn or two of flash to the head area creates a little bright spot to help the fish pick it out from the crowd, and it too is covered by the body material for durability. (Micro tubing is an inexpensive plastic tubing that stretches down incredibly small and makes perfectly segmented bodies on small flies. It's cheap, easy to work with, comes in a slew of colors, and holds up well to repeated chewings.) I like to use a smooth, flat thread like the 16/0 TMC or the newer 14/0 or 16/0 Veevus threads on flies like this; they maintain a smooth, thin underbody while doing double-duty as the ribbing. It's a pretty crafty little trick to tie a fly this way, if I do say so myself! Spin up a bunch of this fun, simple pattern in small sizes. They just might save your day!

SPARKLE MIDGE PUPA (OLIVE)

Hook: #16-24 TMC 2488
Thread: Light Cahill 16/0 Tiemco or 16/0 Veevus
Body: Olive Hareline Micro Tubing
Rib: Tying thread colored black with a Sharpie
Flash: Opal Mirage Tinsel (small)
Head: Same as rib

SPARKLE MIDGE PUPA (BLACK)

Hook: #16-24 TMC 2488
Thread: Black 16/0 Tiemco or 16/0 Veevus
Body: Black Hareline Micro Tubing
Flash: Opal Mirage Tinsel (small)
Head: Tying thread

1. Start the thread immediately behind the hook eye and build a short thread base about two eye lengths back. Leave the thread hanging in the middle of this thread base.

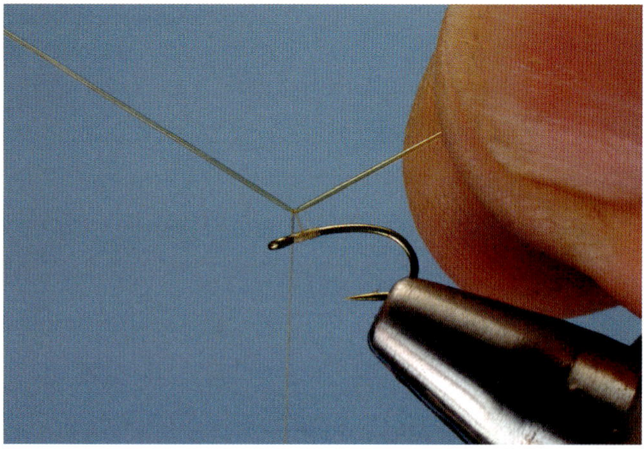

2. Stretch a piece of micro tubing in your fingers tightly to reduce its diameter. This stuff stretches tremendously—pull hard on it. Cross the piece of olive micro tubing under the hook behind the hanging thread. Grab the front end in one hand and the back end in the other and then lift them up from the bottom of the hook to the top on the far side. This maneuver will slide the tubing under the thread and catch the end easily, a better method than trying to capture the floppy end with a loose wrap of thread or a pinch wrap. Let the weight of the bobbin pull the thread down on top of the tubing, centering it on top of the hook.

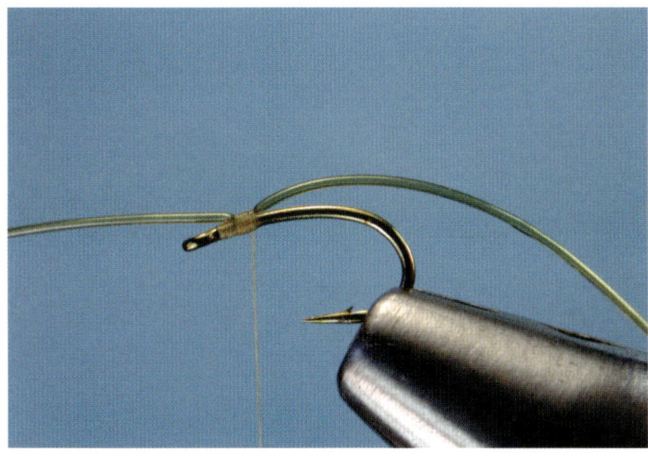

3. Hold the tubing in place and make a tight band of thread over it, working back along the shank to anchor it.

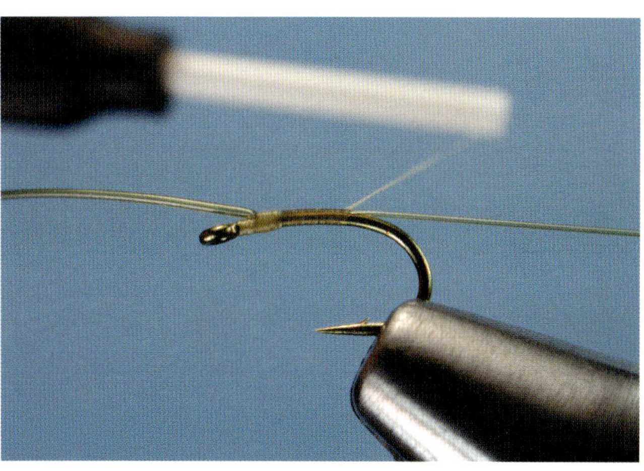

4. Pull hard on the tubing to the rear of the hook and wrap a smooth, even, single layer of tight thread wraps back over it. It helps to hold the tubing slightly toward the near side of the hook as you wrap back over it to allow the thread torque to center it on top of the hook.

5. Before you get all the way down to the bend of the hook, stop and color the thread black with a Sharpie, starting about a half inch from the hook. You should color about three inches or so of thread. You can always color more later if need be, but don't reel any of the colored thread back into your bobbin tip because the ink will smudge off on the bobbin and forever color your light-colored threads (at least until it wears off).

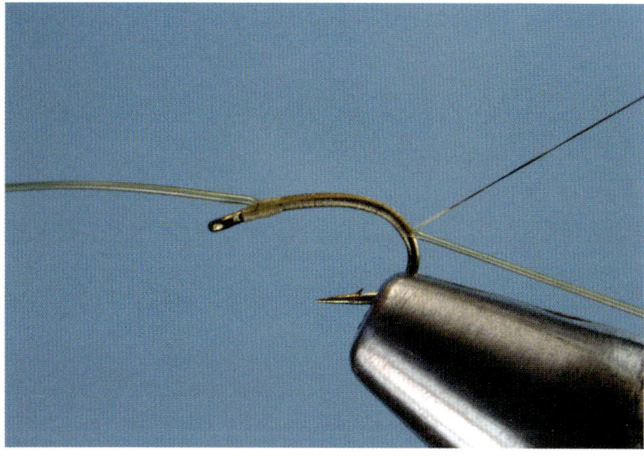

6. Use the remaining light cahill–colored thread to wrap over the tubing to the bend, then spiral forward with the black-colored thread to the hook eye.

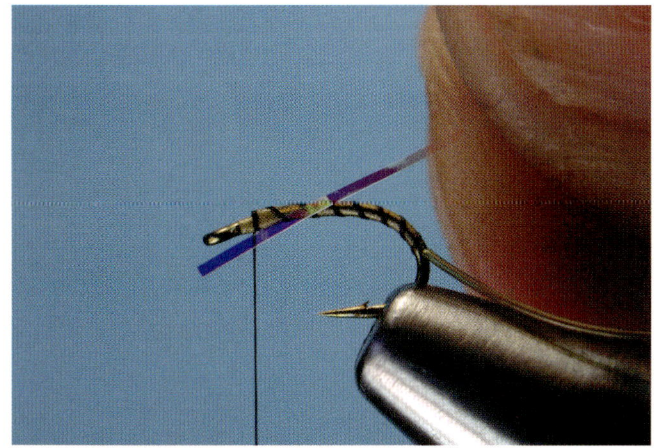

7. Once you've wrapped the rib forward over the underbody, clip the excess tubing off flush at the front of the hook. Lay a piece of small opal Mirage Tinsel in along the near side of the hook shank just behind the tie-in point.

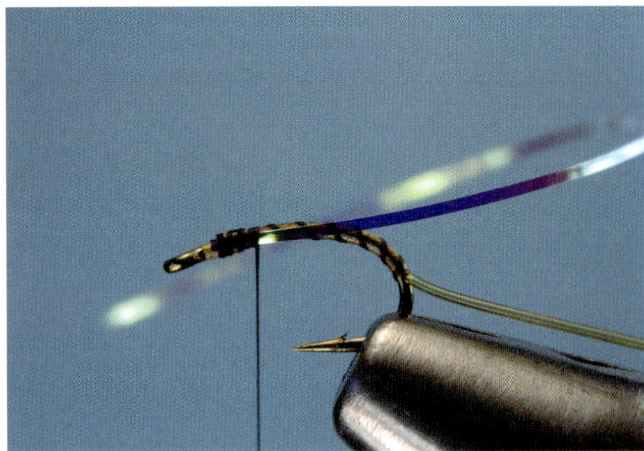

8. Wrap about four even turns of thread back over the tinsel and then bring the thread forward again to the back of the index point. Try to keep this tie-down smooth and level, as that will make wrapping the flash much easier in the next step.

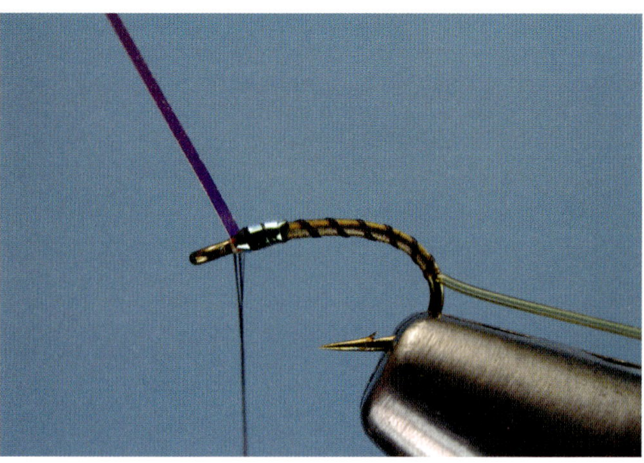

9. Wrap the tinsel forward for about two or three butting turns and tie it off at the back of the index point. These wraps should be as smooth as possible, but the rigid tinsel may want to spread out a bit. A tiny bit of space between the wraps is acceptable here, as they won't show through the finished body.

10. Clip the excess tinsel and make a couple wraps over the stubs to smooth them down.

11. Stretch the micro tubing tightly and wrap it forward over the ribbed thread body as well as the tinsel collar right up to the back of the index point. Make these wraps butt up to one another with no overlap. Tie the tubing off at the hook eye with several firm thread wraps and clip the excess flush against the hook.

12. Use the last of the colored thread to build a rounded thread head at the eye of the hook; whip-finish and clip the thread. If there is any colored thread remaining, clip both it and about three extra inches of thread off the end of the spool. Here, the colored thread crossed over the uncolored thread during the whip-finish and made a mark on the light-colored thread. If you're not careful, the next fly you tie may have a muddy-looking body from this streak of ink on the thread, so it's best to just get into the habit of cutting it off as soon as you finish. Add a tiny drop of head cement to the thread head.

Midges are a mainstay on many spring creeks across the country such as Pennsylvania's Big Spring Creek, where you can catch fish all year long on larva and pupa patterns.

20

SCUD

Scuds are common in still and moving waters across the country and present exciting fishing opportunities when trout key on them. Keeping your patterns sparse and realistic is important to their success.

Scuds are freshwater shrimp commonly found in lakes and river throughout the United States. They are a huge source of protein for trout and where abundant trout feeding on them can grow to epic proportions. Numerous tailwaters across the West, such as the Bighorn and South Platte, have good populations of scuds, and rivers below any type of impoundment often have good populations as well. Having a selection of patterns in various colors and sizes that imitate this important food source is always a good game plan. They range in size from nearly a half-inch long down to about a size 22 hook, although I find that sizes 14 and 16 cover my bases pretty well most of the time.

There are about a million different ways to tie a scud pattern and I think I have played with most of them, but over the years I keep coming back to what I call a Plain Old Scud. No flashback, no weave or bead, no tail or other fanciness—just a plain and simple pattern tied to replicate the real thing.

A multitude of materials that can be used for the shellback on a scud, from

While some anglers go crazy with the color variations, I carry only a few, including a few different shades of olive and orange.

Thin Skin to elastic Scud Back to foils and tinsels and even simple strips of plastic baggie. For the past decade or so I have taken a liking to using an old material called Swiss Straw, a synthetic raffia that, when wet, has a pliable, rubbery look that matches the carapace of a real scud. By tying in a wider-than-usual strip, I allow the Swiss Straw to crinkle up and wrinkle across the back of the fly, which lends some variegation and subtle mottling to the shell.

Almost any coarse dubbing can be used for the body, although not surprisingly, Wapsi's Sow Scud Dubbing seems to work wonderfully. The only downside to this mix of Antron, rabbit fur, opossum, and some other synthetic fibers is that it comes out of the package a little long for the size range of most scuds. Tying with it in its raw form will yield legs that when brushed out are simply too long and require trimming; that creates a square edge across the legs, which just bugs the crap out of me. To better utilize this dubbing for smaller-sized flies, I simply pick up a clump of dubbing and cut it into about quarter- to half-inch sections. Shortening the staple length of the dubbing in this manner will still allow it to wrap tightly around the thread while maintaining the ability to be shagged out to create appropriate-sized legs on these patterns.

While most of the live scuds I find here in Colorado are a smoky olive/gray color, tan and even pale gold colors are common as well. Like so many other underwater critters, scuds take on the color of their surroundings and the lake or river bottom will give you a big clue as to what color the local residents might be. You may also find scuds in a wide range of shades of orange, rust, and pink as well, although these scuds are dead or dying and changing color in the process. Fish are not picky and will eat the dead ones ravenously at times, and a selection of flies tied in these corresponding colors will round out your scud box well. I recall getting orders for scuds from a group of guys when I was a kid, all tied on size 14 hooks in about thirty different colors. These guys were adamant that the exact shade made a difference every time, a conviction I am not prone to myself, but they ordered lots of flies and I am sure I still have the index cards with the dubbing recipes and samples for all the shades somewhere in my tying room. In my experience, you really don't need every single shade; a few well-chosen colors based on the areas you fish should suffice.

I have mentioned before that sight-fishing is one of my favorite things to do, and when given a clear mountain lake with some fish cruising near the shore, tying a lightly weighted scud onto my leader is one of the first things I'll do. The weight helps get the fly down into the fish's path more quickly and allows me to cast a bit closer to the fish and anticipate his direct path a touch more accurately. Often I'll cast well ahead of a cruising fish and let the fly settle to the bottom in the shallow water along the shore. When the fish gets close, I'll simply make a few short strips to hop the scud off the bottom or out of the weeds; more often than not, this is met with a flip of the tail and a crushing strike, all recorded by my mental video camera for replaying during long, boring phone calls or meetings.

SCUD

Hook: #10-20 TMC 2487 or 2457
Weight: Lead or nonlead wire (optional)
Thread: Olive dun 8/0 Uni
Antennae: Dyed olive mallard flank
Rib: 6X mono tippet
Shellback: Olive Swiss Straw
Body: Smoky olive Sow Scud Dubbing

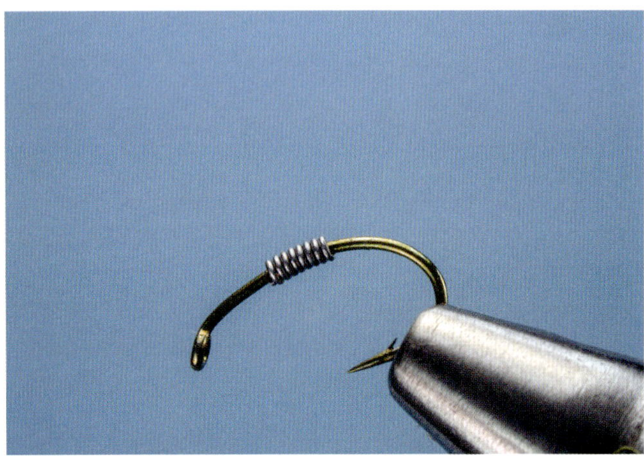

1. Place the hook in the vise, but rather than squaring it up, mount it with the eye tilted down slightly to expose more of the hook bend. We want to use the hook's curvature on this pattern so access to the bend will be important for the next few steps. Make six or eight wraps of lead wire in the center of the shank. The lead not only adds weight to the fly but will also help to shape the body.

2. Start the thread in front of the lead wraps. Build a small thread dam tapering up from the bare shank to the lead, then continue back over the lead wraps and build another thread dam at the back end. Keep wrapping the thread back down the hook bend to cover some of the curve.

3. Select a dyed mallard flank feather with fine tips and preen the fibers out so the tips are somewhat even. Peel the clump of mallard from the stem.

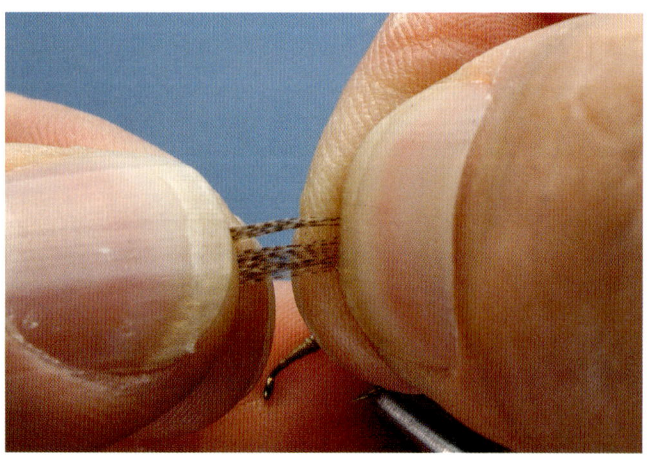

4. Using your thumbnail, break off the fine tips of the mallard fibers.

5. Breaking about a quarter inch of the tips will leave you with a fine-tipped clump that is still slightly ragged, but with a bit thicker fibers that will be more durable on the finished fly. The natural tips of the mallard fibers are delicate and break off easily when the pattern is fished.

6. Take the broken clump of fibers and roll them in your fingertips so they splay out. Measure the tips against the hook shank so they are about half a shank in length.

7. Tie the mallard tips in on top of the shank at the hook bend with a narrow band of thread. The tail (antennae, really, as scuds are generally tied backward on the hook) should splay out at the bend. Resist the urge to wrap over the tails and down around the curve of the hook. You want to stay about even with the hook eye on the back of the hook; while wrapping farther down the bend will create a fly with more of an arched look, you run the risk of eliminating the practical use of the hook bend, which is to hold the fish!

8. Clip the butt ends of the mallard flank at the back end of the lead wraps. Cut a length of 6X tippet and lay it in at the hook bend on top of the shank.

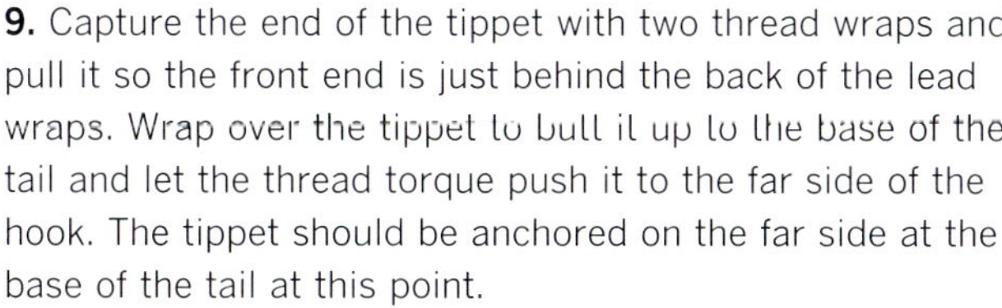

9. Capture the end of the tippet with two thread wraps and pull it so the front end is just behind the back of the lead wraps. Wrap over the tippet to butt it up to the base of the tail and let the thread torque push it to the far side of the hook. The tippet should be anchored on the far side at the base of the tail at this point.

10. Cut a three-inch-long section of Swiss Straw from the card. Swiss Straw comes rolled up into a sort of rope, but you can unroll it into a crinkled sheet (this is what I use for a standard scud back). Unroll the rope into a flattened sheet.

11. Snip the end of the sheet into a strip that is about as wide as the hook gap. Peel the snipped section off the side of the sheet, leaving a long strip of Swiss Straw. You can just tear it lengthwise without having to use your scissors; don't worry about it being perfectly even. Swiss Straw is incredibly strong in cross section, but tears easily along its length.

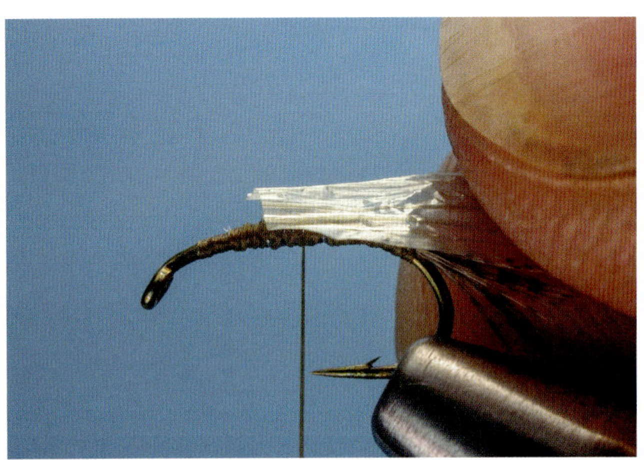

12. Lay the Swiss Straw in on top of the shank with the thread hanging in the middle of the hook. Put your material hand thumb down on top of it to hold it flat against the shank.

13. Capture the end of the straw with a few turns of thread in the middle of the hook.

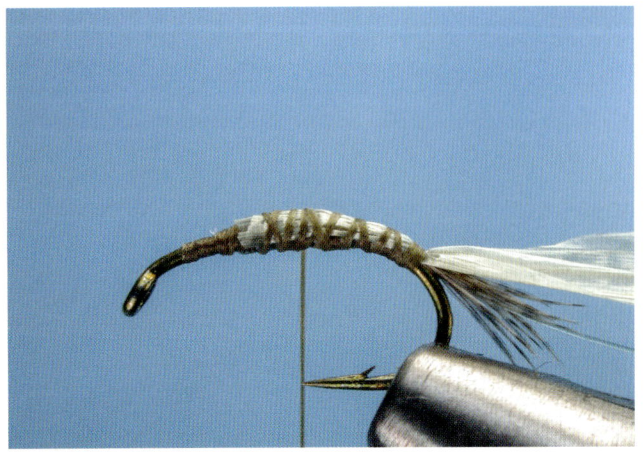

14. Pull down on the Swiss Straw at the hook bend and wrap the thread back over it to the base of the tail. We want the straw to buckle around the hook shank and cup up against it. Swiss Straw becomes slimy looking and pliable when wet and creates a wonderful back on a fly like this. It's cheap, easy, and often overlooked—but it's hard to beat when it comes to realism.

15. I really like Wapsi Sow Scud Dubbing but find the fibers a bit long for many applications. I don't want my scuds to have legs that are an inch and a half long, so I pull out a loose clump of dubbing and cut it in half or in thirds to shorten the staple length of the fibers and make them more appropriately sized for the hook. I find this also make the fibers easier to dub. Don't chop the dubbing up, just cut the clump straight across in half or in thirds.

16. Apply a thin, tight strand of Sow Scud Dubbing to the thread. Even though we are going to later pick this dubbing out, we want the dubbing applied tightly because it will hold its shape much better this way. Try to keep the ends of the dubbing strand as tight and thin as you can to aid in building the body taper.

17. Begin wrapping the dubbing at the base of the tail. Again, try to keep the dubbing here thin. Ultimately we want a football- shaped body, with the ends small in diameter and with the middle as the fattest part. It makes sense to start off thin because that will give us some leeway on building the taper toward the center, whereas if we make the ends too fat to begin with, the whole fly is going to come out too fat as well.

18. Continue dubbing forward to the index point, creating an elongated, football-shaped body. You'll need to overlap a few turns at the center of the body to achieve the right shape and taper down again toward the hook eye. You can see here the eclectic mix of fibers used in the Sow Scud Dubbing: opossum, Antron, rabbit fur, and Himalayan bat all combine to great effect in a fly like this.

19. Flatten out the Swiss Straw and pull it forward over the top of the fly, letting it pull down along the sides of the hook.

20. Catch the end of the Swiss Straw with two turns at the hook eye. You can see the crinkled texture of the shellback here as it comes over the top of the fly.

21. Spiral-wrap the tippet forward over the body and shellback, pulling hard as you come down on each turn to sink the monofilament into the dubbing. I try to make relatively even and wide segments; if your rib spacing is too tight the mono binds down too much of the dubbing and will make it difficult to pick out later. Tie the mono off at the hook eye with several firm turns of thread and clip the excess as well as the remaining Swiss Straw stub. Incidentally, if we had tied the tippet on the near side, the first turn would lift the edge of the shellback at the bend and muck it up. Simply tying the rib in on the far side results in a cleaner fly.

22. Build a smooth but short thread head and whip-finish.

23. For shagging out a scud pattern, I like to use a strip of the hook side of Velcro. Typically it comes in strips about three-quarters inch wide; cut this in half lengthwise and trim the bare piece off the outside edge. The Velcro makes a perfect tool for working within the hook gap.

24. Place the strip of Velcro bristle-side up under the body of the fly and rake it back and forth like you're doing a shoe-shine. The Velcro will grab the dubbing fibers under the fly and pull them out, creating nice legs. Finish by sweeping this dubbing toward the hook bend with the Velcro strip.

25. The finished legs should be just a touch longer than the hook gap but remain ragged-ended to match the real thing a bit better. If you were to have left the dubbing its normal length, you'd have to trim the legs to length with your scissors and leave square ends, and nobody wants that.

26. Top view of the finished fly.

BEVER'S BETTER BUCKSKIN

A fresh take on an existing pattern, the Better Buckskin tosses a flash back and uniquely made thorax into the mix. Replacing the conventional Buckskin's body of chamois or deer hide with a more durable and easy to use synthetic improves the fly and simplifies the tying process.

Caddis larvae, in various forms, are present in most river systems and often make up a good portion of a trout's diet. They are a commonly available food source that is often overlooked by anglers, but never by the fish. Throughout the year, and particularly in the leaner seasons of winter and early spring, fishing a caddis larva can be the cause of a surprising amount of bent rods.

Free-living caddis resemble tiny caterpillars and, like underwater hobos, they live around and under rocks on the substrate. Others, known as net builders, live in their own little houses built out of a spiderweb-like netting. Still others, known as cased caddis, construct homes of sticks or stones. Caddis larvae are an extremely viable food source for trout and should be among the patterns you carry in your fly box. We've all seen patterns tied to replicate these common insects and a few of us even carry them around in our boxes, but when it comes down to actually fishing them with confidence, I know few anglers who do.

When tying this fly, especially smaller sized specimens, you'll want to be sure to cut the end of the Ultra Suede to a short, pointed tip to reduce the bulk at the tie-in area. I have found that a metal straightedge and a roller cutter work wonderfully and make it easy to produce useable strips even thinner than you'd really ever need.

The Buckskin has been around for a lot of years and I have to admit I caught an awful lot of fish on it back in the day. Traditionally tied with a strip of tanned deer leather wrapped around the hook, many tiers quickly learned that substituting a thinner strip of chamois leather was more appropriate and easier to use on small hooks. One of the inherent problems all tiers have with the Buckskin is getting that strip of leather cut thin enough to produce a realistically sized fly while at the same time being thick enough to not fall apart during the tying process. In my commercial tying days I tied hundreds of Buckskins, and through trial and error finally settled on an elaborate process of wetting the chamois leather, stretching it out flat, and letting it dry before cutting it into thin strips with a razor blade and a straightedge. What should have been a quick and easy fly was compounded into something much more complicated by virtue of the material it was made of.

Then along came my friend Luke Bever. Luke was a big fan of the Buckskin pattern as well but he always felt he could do a little more to better represent a caddis larva, so he started tinkering. The fly that I'll share here is of Luke's design from start to finish. It features a much more realistic thorax and a flashback, but perhaps the biggest improvement was Luke's finding a better material to use for the body itself. He discovered that a thin strip of synthetic Ultra Suede was a perfect chamois substitute. With more stretch, better strength, and a host of available colors, the Ultra Suede has turned out to be the best thing to ever happen to the Buckskin.

Luke's addition of a flashback strip from back to front, a wire rib, and his unique combination of peacock herl and longer ostrich herl create a fly that truly is better than the original and befitting of the name he's given his variation. I have to take a moment here and say how innovative I find the process by which he creates the head. Using the proven fish-attracting allure of peacock herl as a base and combining it with a few spiraled wraps of leggy ostrich herl, this version makes a perfect representation of the head and thorax of a caddis larva, and I'm a little irritated that I didn't come up with this myself. The fly is simple to tie and is a stunning copy of the real thing—perfect.

BEVER'S BETTER BUCKSKIN

Hook: #12-16 TMC 3761
Thread: Black 8/0 Uni
Rib: Brassie or small copper wire
Shellback: Medium pearl or Mirage tinsel
Abdomen: Tan Ultra Suede or chamois
Thorax: Peacock herl and black ostrich herl

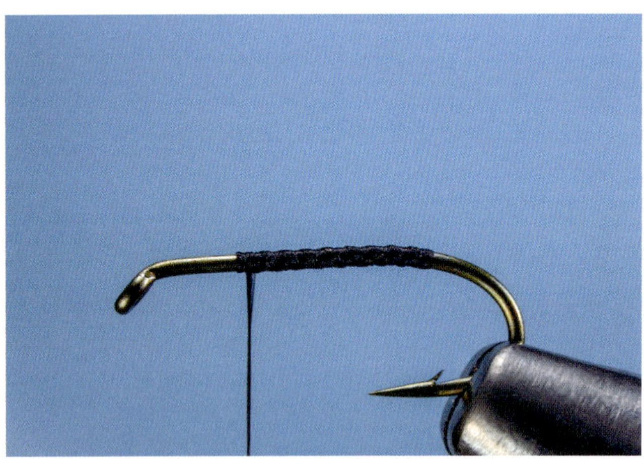

1. Start the thread at the 75 percent point and wrap a thread base back to the bend of the hook. Return the thread to the starting point.

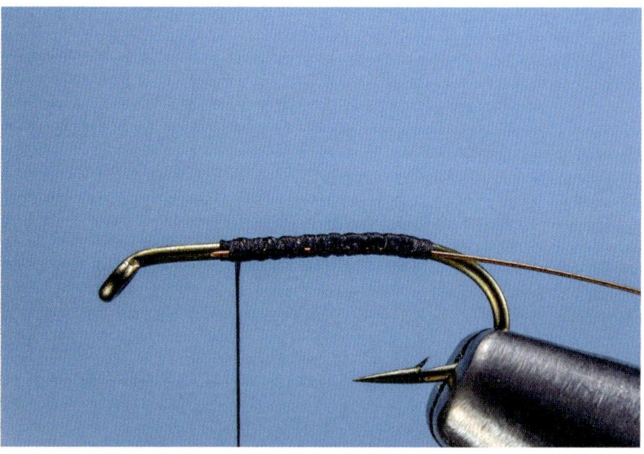

2. Tie in a length of copper wire along the near side of the hook and wrap back over it to the bend. Return the thread to the starting point.

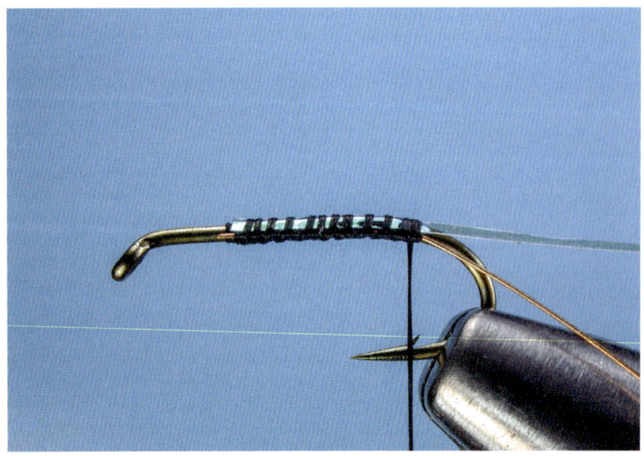

3. Tie in a length of medium pearl tinsel on the top of the hook at the starting point. Wrap back over the tinsel, taking care to keep it centered on the top of the hook, all the way back to the bend.

4. Cut a thin strip of Ultra Suede or chamois and trim the end to a sharp point. Tie the pointed end in right at the bend of the hook with just a few tight, flat wraps so as to not create a lump. Return the thread to the starting point, and then roll the Ultra Suede in your fingertips to twist it up into a cord.

5. Begin wrapping the Ultra Suede forward, rolling it in your fingers as you go to maintain the twist.

6. Tie it off at the 75 percent point.

7. Clip the excess Ultra Suede and build a thread base up to the hook eye and back again to the front of the abdomen.

8. Tie in a single strand of black ostrich by its butt end at the front of the abdomen.

9. Then tie in two thick strands of peacock herl by their tips right in front of the ostrich. Move the thread to the index point just behind the eye.

10. Make two or three turns with the peacock herl up to the eye and tie them off. Clip the excess herl flush.

11. Now wrap the ostrich forward through the peacock herl with two or three well-spaced turns. Tie the ostrich off at the index point and clip the excess.

12. Wet your fingers a bit and sweep the ostrich and peacock herl down and to the sides of the thorax.

13. Pull the pearl tinsel forward over the top of the fly tightly.

14. Tie the tinsel down just behind the hook eye with three tight turns of thread. Make sure the tinsel is centered across the top of the fly and that it is pushing the peacock and ostrich down and to the sides.

15. Wrap the copper wire ribbing forward over the abdomen to the back of the thorax with open turns. Bring the last wrap of ribbing under the thorax and tie it off on the near side of the hook just behind the eye. Helicopter the end of the wire to break it off.

16. Clip the excess tinsel as well at this point and build a small thread head over the stubs. Whip-finish and clip the thread.

17. A variation with chartreuse wire for the ribbing.

TOP 30 NYMPHS

Most great anglers have simplified their fly selection, or at least simplified their core group of patterns, to flies that they are confident in. Over time, you will come up with your own list, which may even include flies of your own design.

Choosing the top ten, or twenty, or even thirty nymph patterns would be a neverending job. Given flits of mood, location, and water conditions, this list could and does change for me on a week-by-week basis. In addition to the flies covered in the chapters of this book, the patterns listed here are all ones that I have grown confident in over the years. Some of them no longer reside in my fly box due to being pushed out by something newer, flashier, or just plain more compelling to me. The one bit of advice I can offer on this is to try everything, both from a tying and a fishing standpoint. I've never been sorry that I added a technique to my tying repertoire nor a pattern to my fly box. This is not to say that I have loved everything that's ever gone into doing this, but the experience with both tying and fishing a variety of patterns is invaluable. Now get to work.

EGAN'S IRON LOTUS

Hook: #14 Umpqua Competition C400BL
Bead: Gold tungsten slotted bead (3 mm)
Weight: .015" lead wire
Tail: Medium Pardo Coq de Leon Fibers
Abdomen: Olive 70-denier UTC
Rib: White 6/0 Uni
Coating: Clear Cure Goo Hydro
Thorax Thread: Red 70-denier UTC
Wing case: Black Wapsi Flashback Tinsel or black Thin Skin
Thorax: Natural Arizona Synthetic Peacock Dubbing

TUNGSTONE (GOLDEN)

Hook: #4-12 TMC 5262
Bead: Gold tungsten
Thread: Yellow 6/0 Danville
Tail: Gold goose biots
Rib: 3X mono
Flashback: Pearl Lateral Scale
Shellback: Mottled bustard Thin Skin
Abdomen: Tan Wapsi Sow Scud Dubbing
Legs: Gold dyed grizzly hen saddle
Wing cases: Mottled bustard Thin Skin
Thorax: Tan Wapsi Sow Scud Dubbing

POISON TUNG (BLUE)

Hook: #16-20 TMC 2488
Bead: Silver tungsten (2 mm)
Thread: Gray 8/0 Uni
Rib: Blue UTC Wire (small)
Head: Lavender UV Ice Dub

FLASH JUJUBEE MIDGE (CHARTREUSE)

Hook: #18-22 TMC 2488
Thread: 16/0 white under abdomen and 16/0 black for thorax
Abdomen: Two strands chartreuse Super Hair and one strand black Super Hair
Wing case: White Fluoro Fibre
Thorax: 1/100" Mirage Flashabou
Wingbuds: Leftover ends of Fluoro Fibre wingcase

AP NYMPH

Hook: #14-18 TMC 3761
Thread: Iron Dun 8/0 Uni
Tail: Moose body hair
Rib: Copper wire (X small)
Abdomen: Natural dark gray muskrat dubbing
Wing case/Legs: Moose body hair
Thorax: Same as abdomen

RANDY'S BAETIS

Hook: #16-22 TMC 101
Thread: Camel 8/0 Uni
Tail: Brown partridge fibers
Rib: Copper wire (X small)
Abdomen: Khaki brown beaver dubbing
Legs: Brown partridge fibers
Wing case: Tyvek strip colored with black Sharpie
Thorax: Khaki brown beaver dubbing

RAINBOW WARRIOR

Hook: #14-20 TMC 2457
Thread: Red 8/0 Uni
Bead: Silver tungsten, sized to hook
Tail: Natural pheasant tail fibers
Abdomen: Medium pearl tinsel
Wing case: Medium pearl tinsel
Thorax: Rainbow Sow Scud Dubbing

MERCER'S POXY-BACK GOLDEN STONE

Hook: #6-16 TMC 5262
Thread: Yellow 70-denier UTC
Bead: Gold-colored brass or tungsten, sized to hook
Tails/Antennae: Gold turkey biots
Weight: Lead wire along sides of hook shank
Abdomen: Sulphur orange turkey biots (usually at least two)
Wing cases: Mottled turkey tail quill slips (two), coated with Clear Cure Goo or epoxy
Thorax: Golden stone Mercer's Buggy Nymph Dubbing or tan Wapsi Sow Scud Dubbing
Legs: Mottled hen saddle feather

HALFBACK

Hook: #4-14 TMC 5262
Thread: 3/0 Monocord or 8/0 Uni (depending on fly size)
Weight: Lead wire
Tail: Natural pheasant tail fibers
Shellback: Natural pheasant tail fibers
Hackle: Soft brown rooster saddle
Abdomen: Peacock herl
Thorax: Peacock herl

KAUFMANN'S STONE

Hook: #2-12 TMC 300
Thread: 3/0 Monocord
Weight: .025" lead wire
Tail: Brown goose biots
Rib: Brown D-Rib (small)
Abdomen: Brown seal fur sub, Angora goat, or coarse synthetic dubbing
Wing cases: Natural turkey tail sections
Thorax: Same as abdomen
Antennae: Brown goose biots

BIOT EPOXY STONE (BLACK)

Hook: #6-12 TMC 5263
Bead: Black brass or tungsten, sized to hook
Weight: Lead wire, sized to hook
Thread: Black 70-denier UTC
Tail: Black turkey biot
Abdomen: Black turkey biots
Flash: Single strand pearl Flashabou
Wing case: Black Thin Skin, coated with epoxy
Thorax: Coarse black dubbing
Legs: Soft grizzly hen saddle fibers
Antennae: Black turkey biots

BITCH CREEK NYMPH

Hook: #4-12 TMC 5263
Thread: Black 8/0 Uni
Tail and Antennae: White round rubber legs (medium)
Rib: Copper wire
Abdomen: Fluorescent fire orange chenille
Shellback: Black chenille
Hackle: Soft black rooster saddle
Thorax: Black chenille
Note: In smaller sizes from #10 down, use Ultra Chenille in place of conventional rayon chenille as its density and smaller size works better for smaller flies.

MERCER'S PSYCHO PRINCE

Hook: #12-18 TMC 3769
Bead: Gold brass or tungsten, sized to hook
Weight: Lead wire, sized to hook
Thread: Camel 8/0 Uni
Tail: Brown goose biots
Rib: Copper wire
Shellback: Natural turkey wing
Abdomen: Olive Ice Dub
Wing: Electric yellow Angel Hair
Legs: White goose biot
Head: Brown Ice Dub

TUNG TEASER

Hook: #10-18 TMC 5262
Thread: Black 8/0 Uni
Bead: Gold tungsten, sized to hook
Tail: White goose biots
Rib: Gold UTC wire
Abdomen: Bronze peacock Arizona Synthetic Dubbing
Flash: Single strand pearl Flashabou
Wing case: Mottled natural bustard Thin Skin
Legs: Natural brown mottled India hen saddle

TWO-BIT HOOKER (BLACK)

Hook: #14-18 TMC 3769
Beads: Two 3/32" black tungsten beads for #14, two 5/64" for #16, and two 1/16" for #18
Thread: Black 16/0 Veevus
Tails: Black India hen saddle fibers
Abdomen: Tying thread
Rib: Fine copper wire
Wing case: Opal Mirage Tinsel (medium)
Thorax: Black Superfine
Legs: Black India hen saddle fibers
Coating: Clear Cure Goo Tack Free Brushable

TUNGSTEN JUJUBAETIS (RED)

Hook: #16-22 TMC 2488
Bead: Copper tungsten (1.5 mm)
Thread: White 16/0 under abdomen and black 8/0 under thorax
Tail: Mottled brown India hen saddle fibers
Abdomen: 2 strands red and 1 strand dark brown Super Hair
Flash: Medium Opal Mirage Tinsel
Wing case/Legs: Brown Fluoro Fibre
Thorax: Black tying thread
Coating: Clear Cure Goo Tack Free Brushable

WONDER NYMPH

Hook: #16-22 TMC 2487
Thread: Gray 8/0 Uni
Tail: Blue dun hen hackle fibers
Abdomen: Olive goose biot
Wing case: Fluffy base of blue dun hen neck feather
Thorax: Olive gray Superfine

MERCURY ZEBRA MIDGE

Hook: #16-22 TMC 2487
Thread: Black 70-denier UTC
Bead: Glass Mercury Bead (X small)
Rib: Silver UTC Wire (X small)
Body: Black tying thread
Head: Black Superfine Dubbing

SOFT-HACKLE EMERGER

Hook: #16-22 TMC 101
Thread: Gray Uni 8/0
Tail: Three strands white Fluoro Fibre
Abdomen: Gray muskrat or beaver dubbing
Hackle: Medium dun hen neck
Wing: White Fluoro Fibre
Thorax: Gray muskrat or beaver dubbing

GRAPHIC CADDIS

Hook: #14-18 TMC 2499SP-BL
Thread: Olive 70-denier UTC
Abdomen: Olive Micro Tubing
Tag: Silver holographic Flashabou
Collar: Natural Hungarian partridge fibers
Head: Natural gray ostrich herl

While some anglers go crazy with the color variations of RS2s, I carry only a few, including a few different shades of olive.

RS2

Hook: #16-24 TMC 101
Thread: Gray 8/0 Uni
Tail: White Microfibetts
Abdomen and thorax: Gray Superfine
Wing: White Antron yarn

MIRACLE NYMPH

Hook: #16-24 TMC 2487
Thread: White 70-denier UTC
Rib: Fine copper wire
Head: White tying thread colored with black Sharpie

TELLICO NYMPH

Hook: #10-18 TMC 3761
Thread: Black 8/0 Uni
Weight: Lead wire, sized to hook
Tail: Barred teal flank
Shellback: Natural turkey wing quill section coated with Clear Cure Goo
Rib: Peacock herl twisted with fine copper wire
Body: Yellow rayon floss
Hackle: Brown hen neck

CDC PHEASANT TAIL

Hook: #10-16 TMC 5262
Bead: Gold or copper tungsten, sized to hook
Weight: Lead wire, sized to hook
Thread: Rusty brown 70-denier UTC or 8/0 Uni in smaller hook sizes
Tail: Dyed orange ring-necked pheasant tail fibers
Flashback: Pearl Flashabou
Abdomen: Dyed orange ring-necked pheasant tail fibers
Rib: Copper wire or hot orange UTC wire
Wing case: Pearl Lagartun Mini Flat Braid
Thorax: Peacock herl
Collar: Natural dun CDC

ZUG BUG

Hook: #10-18 TMC 3761
Thread: Black 8/0 Uni
Weight: Lead wire, sized to hook
Tail: Peacock sword fibers
Rib: Silver wire or oval tinsel
Body: Peacock herl
Hackle: Brown hen neck
Wing case: Mallard flank dyed wood duck gold

BIRD'S NEST

Hook: #14-20 TMC 3761
Thread: Tan 8/0 Uni
Tail: Mallard flank dyed tan
Abdomen: Dark tan Superfine or hare's mask
Rib: Fine copper wire
Collar: Mallard flank dyed tan
Head: Same as abdomen

CASED CADDIS

Hook: #12-20 TMC 3761
Thread: Black 8/0 Uni
Bead: Black tungsten, sized to hook
Weight: Lead wire
Rib: Fine copper wire
Case: Natural mottled turkey tail fibers, wrapped
Thorax: Caddis green beaver dubbing
Legs: Black India hen saddle fibers

STICK-CASED CADDIS

Hook: #12-20 TMC 3761
Thread: Black 8/0 Uni
Bead: Black tungsten, sized to hook
Weight: Lead wire, sized to hook
Rib: Brown hackle feather, wrapped and clipped short
Case: Peacock herl
Thorax: Chartreuse Ice Dub
Head: Peacock Ice Dub

NET BUILDER

Hook: #16-20 Partridge Klinkhammer
Thread: Black 8/0 Uni
Bead: Black tungsten
Weight: .010" lead wire
Tail: White CDC, clipped short
Rib: 4X tippet
Shellback: Olive Flyspecks Thin Skin
Abdomen: Olive Nature's Spirit Emerger Dubbing
Thorax: Olive brown Nature's Spirit Emerger Dubbing

SKINNY NELSON

Hook: #16-20 TMC 3761
Bead: Black tungsten, sized to hook
Thread: Black 70-denier UTC
Tail: Natural ringneck pheasant tail fibers
Rib: Gold UTC Wire (x-small)
Wing case: Pearl Flashabou
Thorax: Peacock herl

FLY PATTERN INDEX

** Pages on which tying sequences appear are in bold*